Faces

A COLORING BOOK
BY ALEX CARRILLO

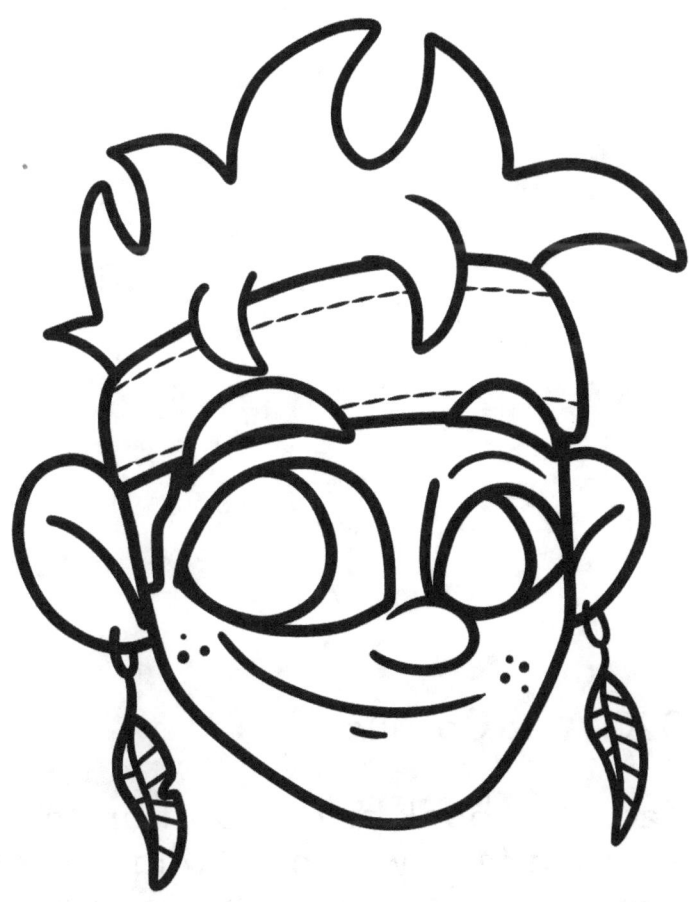

TRANSLATED BY
GRACIA EMMA DE LA FUENTE

This book is dedicated to all the people that have supported my art through this incredible journey: my family, friends, and the amazing art community.

Boost your creativity, relax and enjoy FACES.

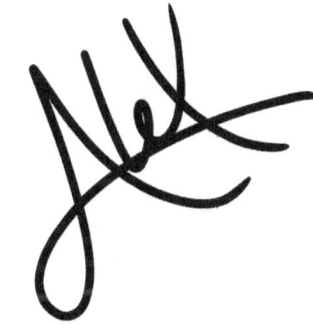

- Alex Carrillo

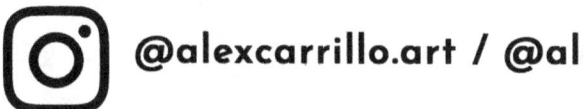 @alexcarrillo.art / @alexcarrillof

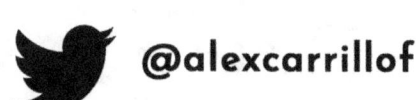 @alexcarrillof

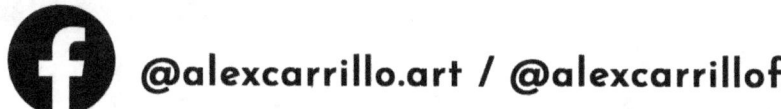 @alexcarrillo.art / @alexcarrillof

Faces

THIS COLORING BOOK BELONGS TO:

_____

TEST YOUR COLORS
ON THIS PAGE

TEST YOUR COLORS
ON THIS PAGE

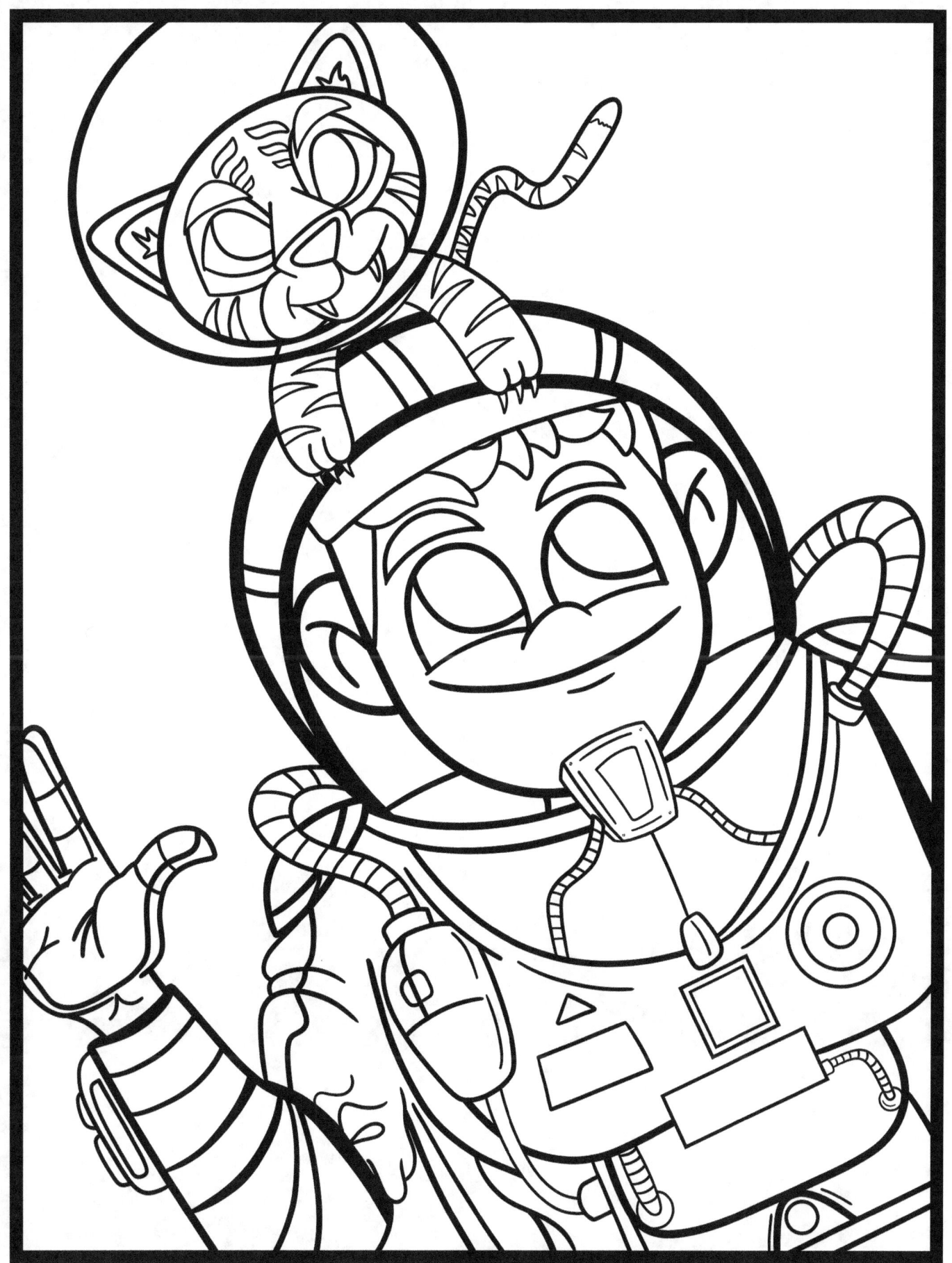

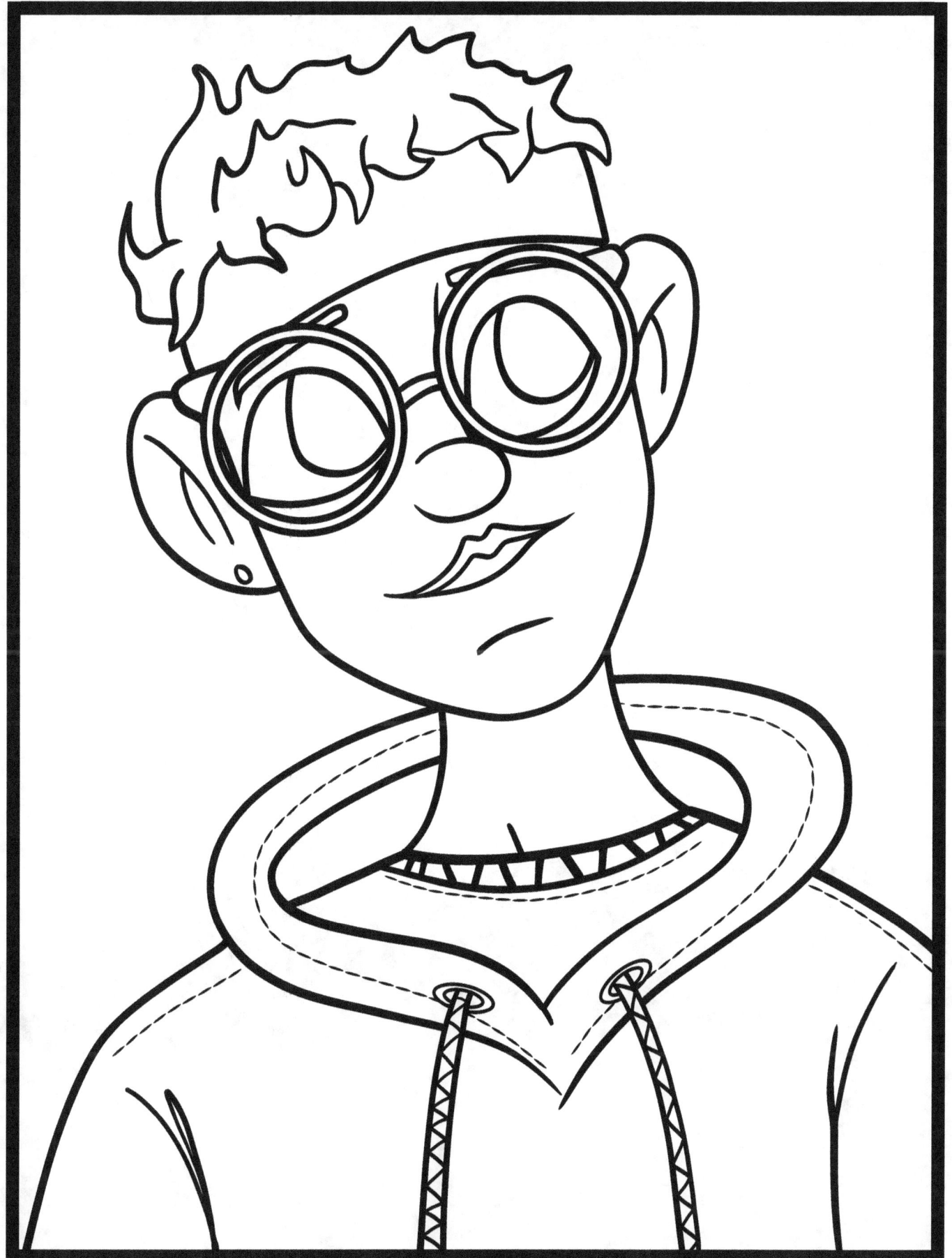

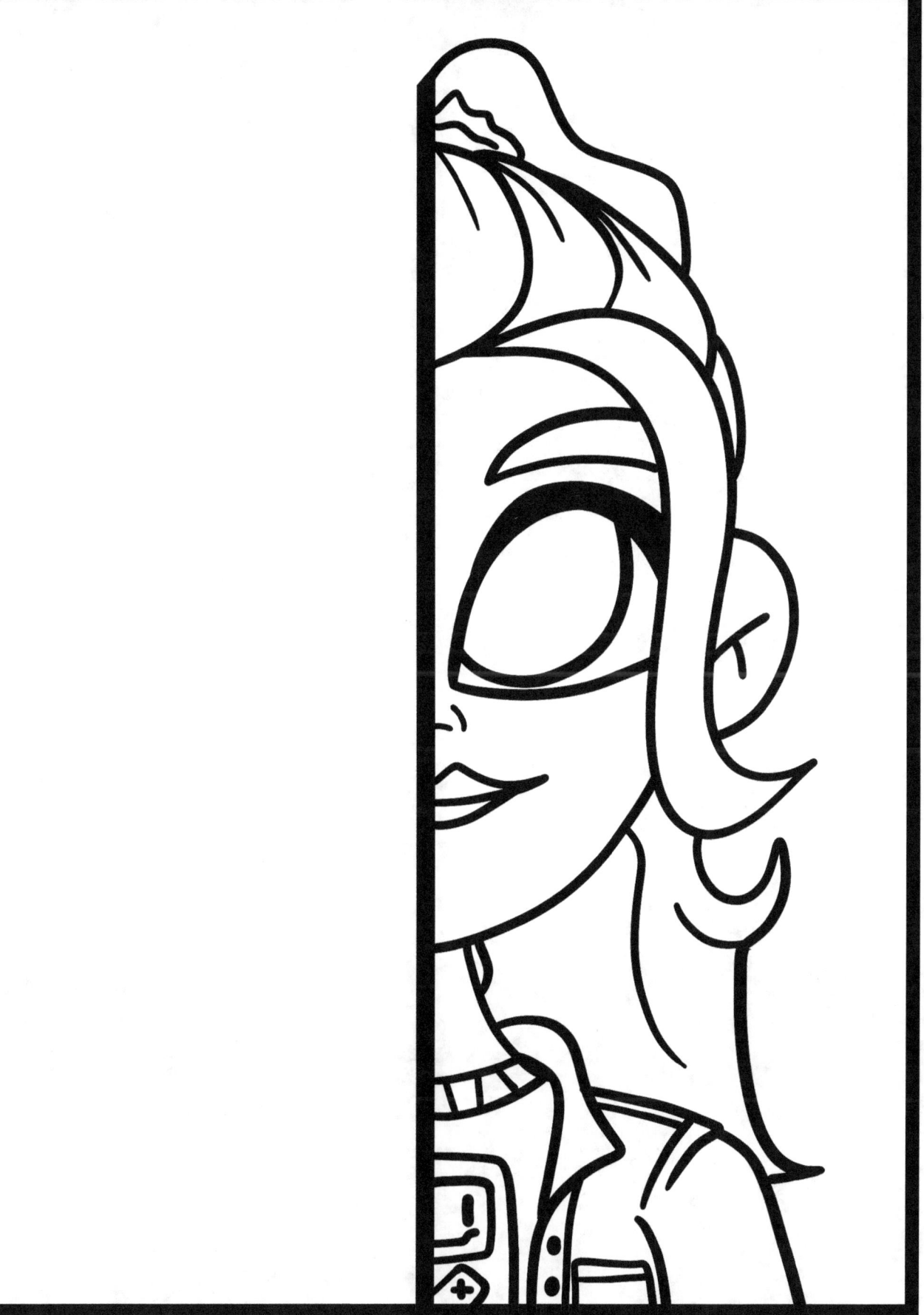

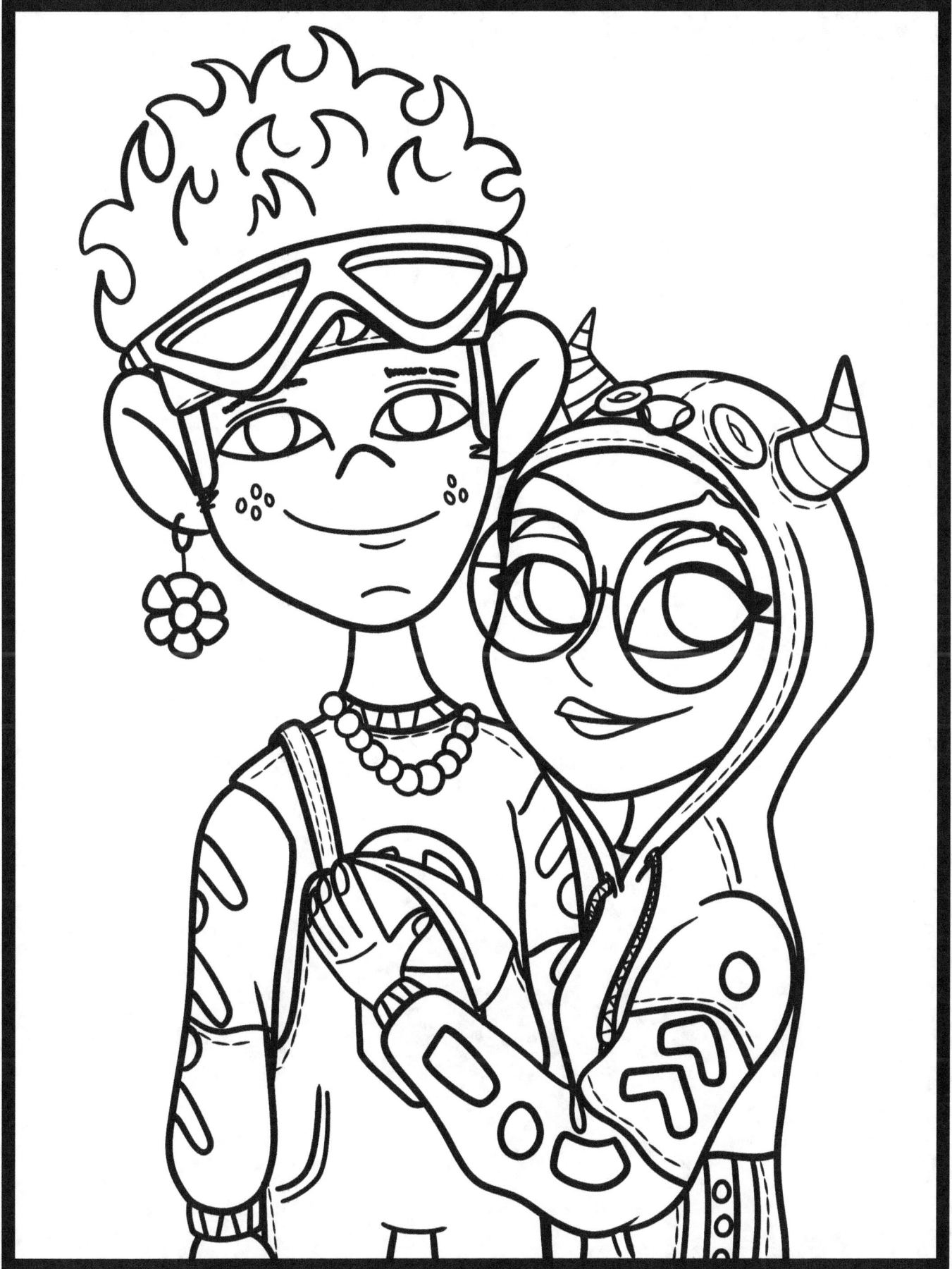

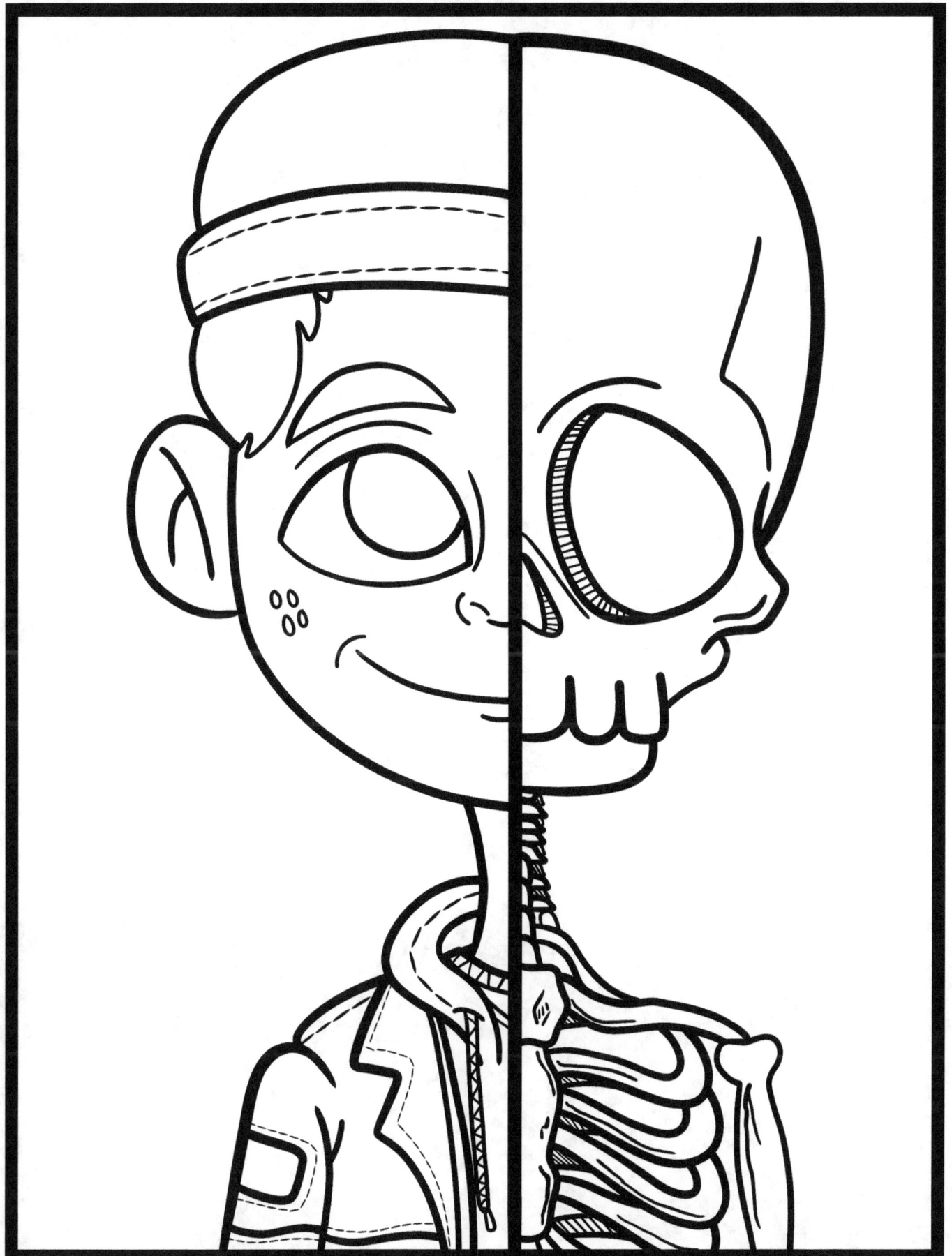

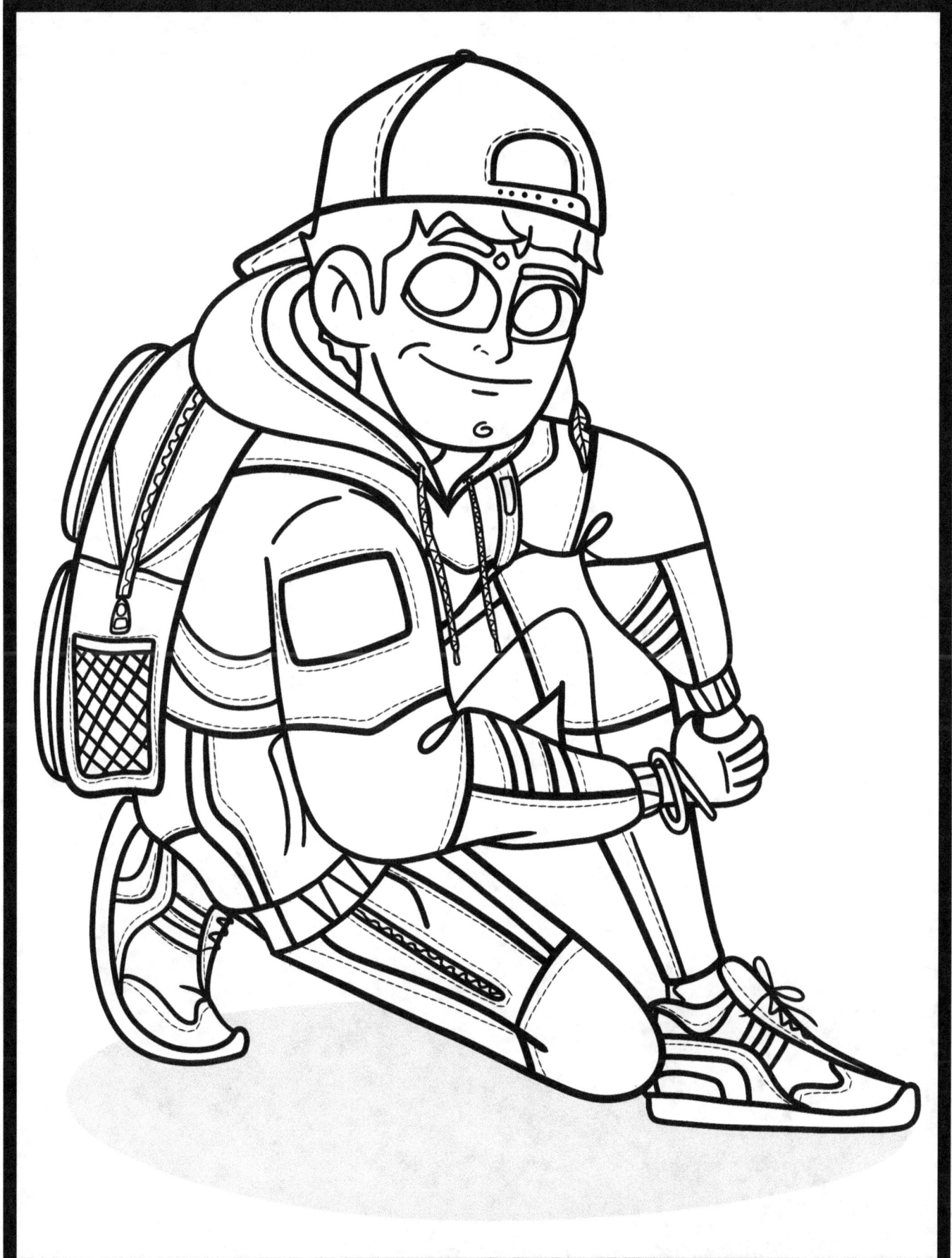

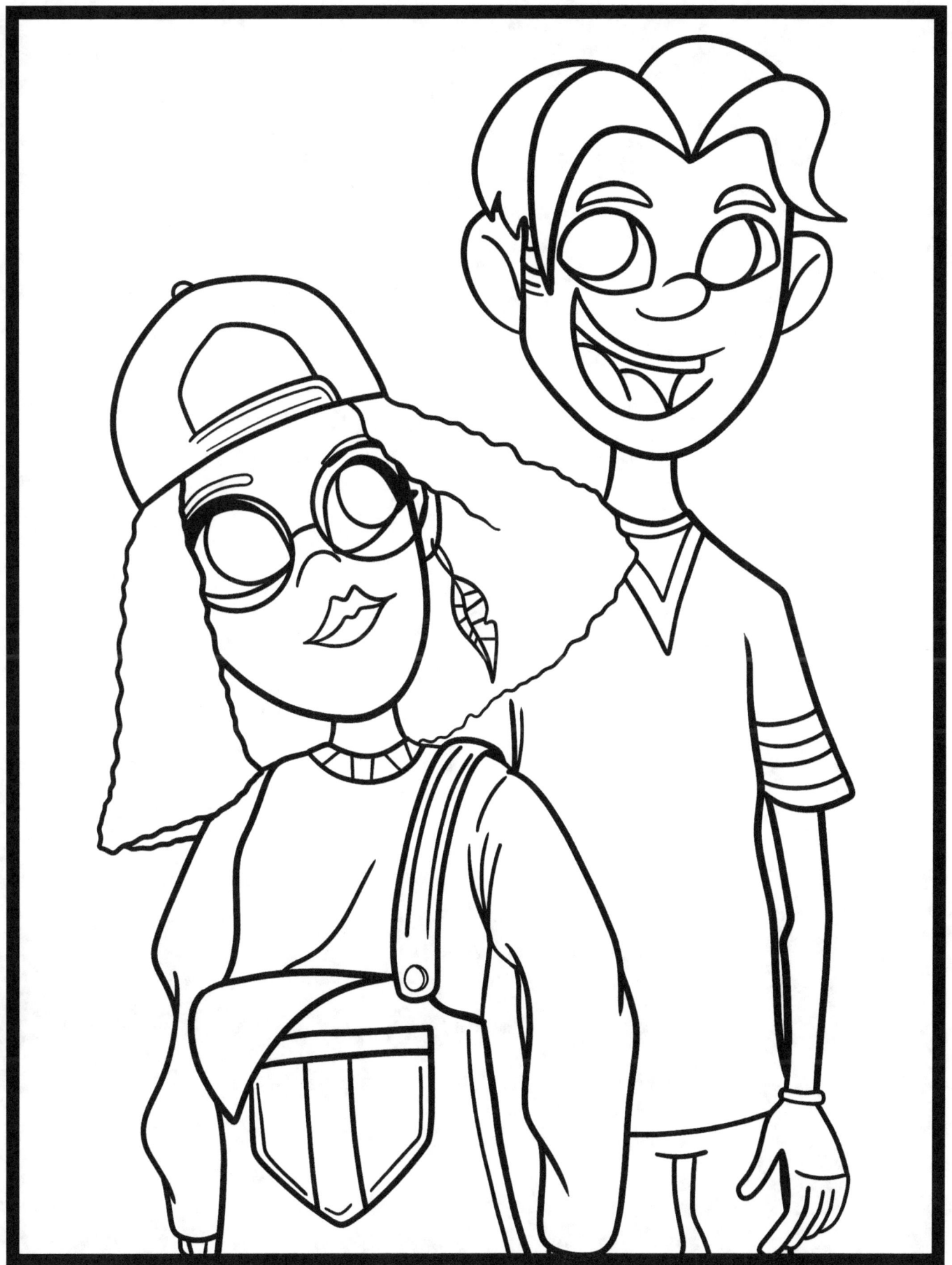

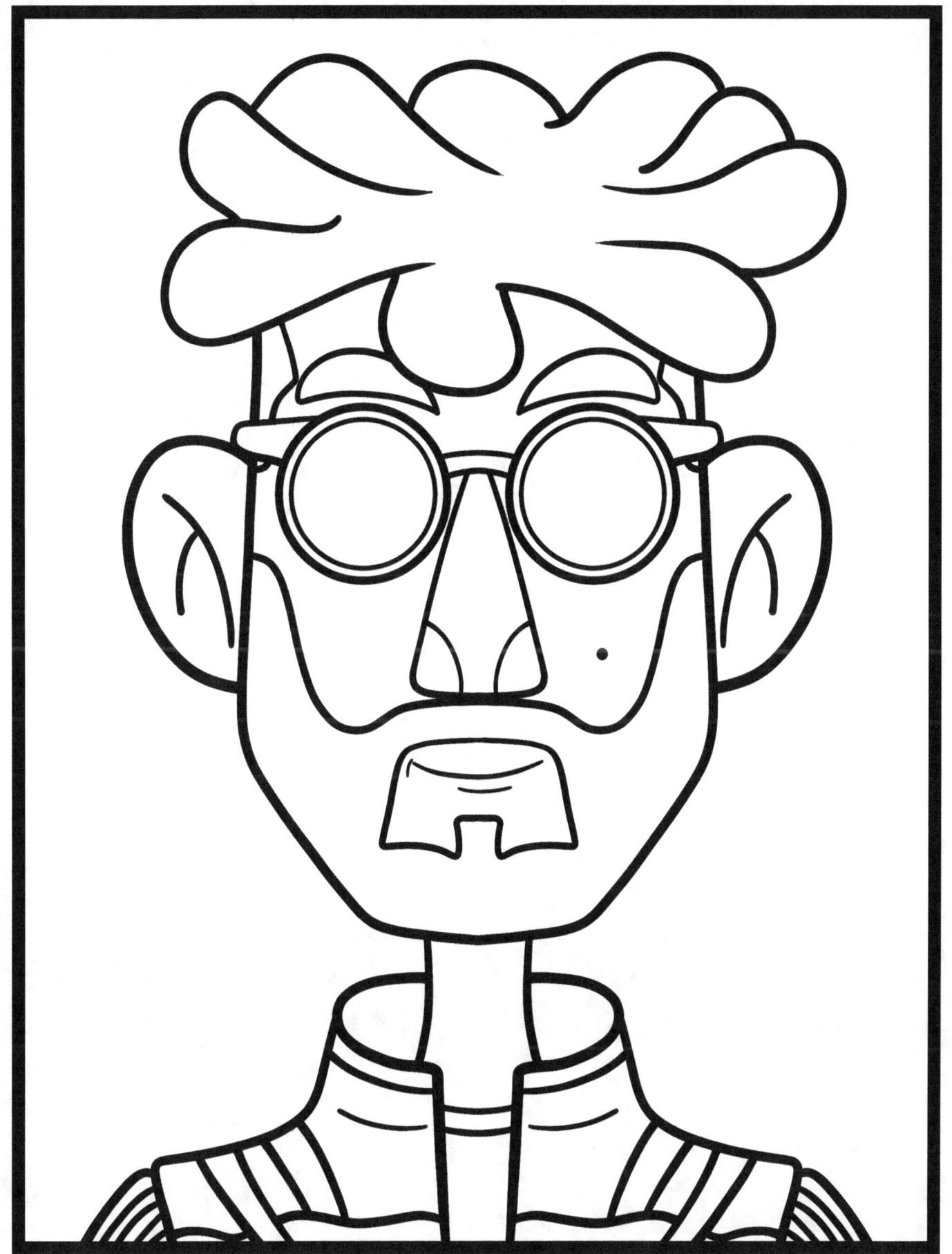

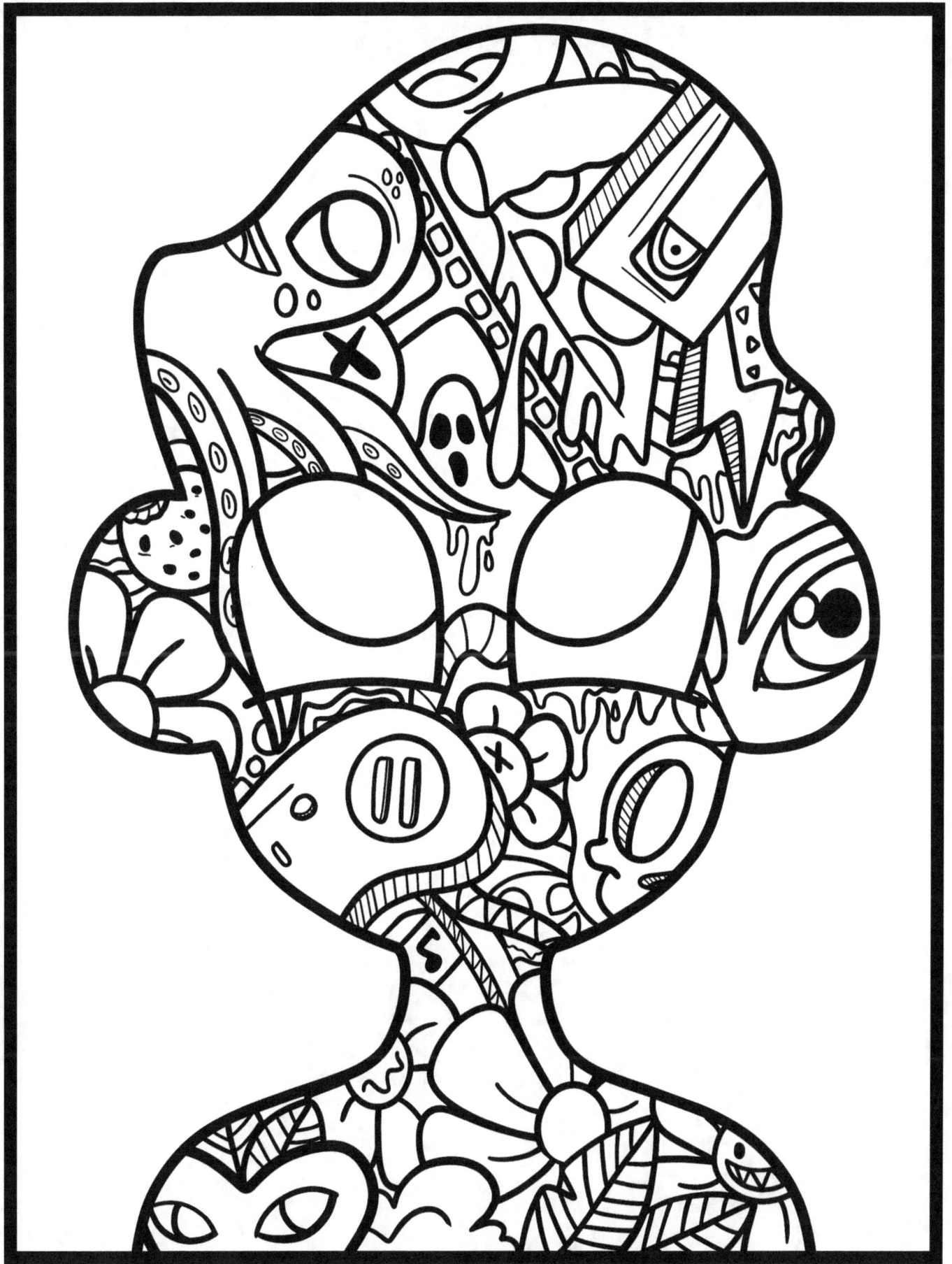

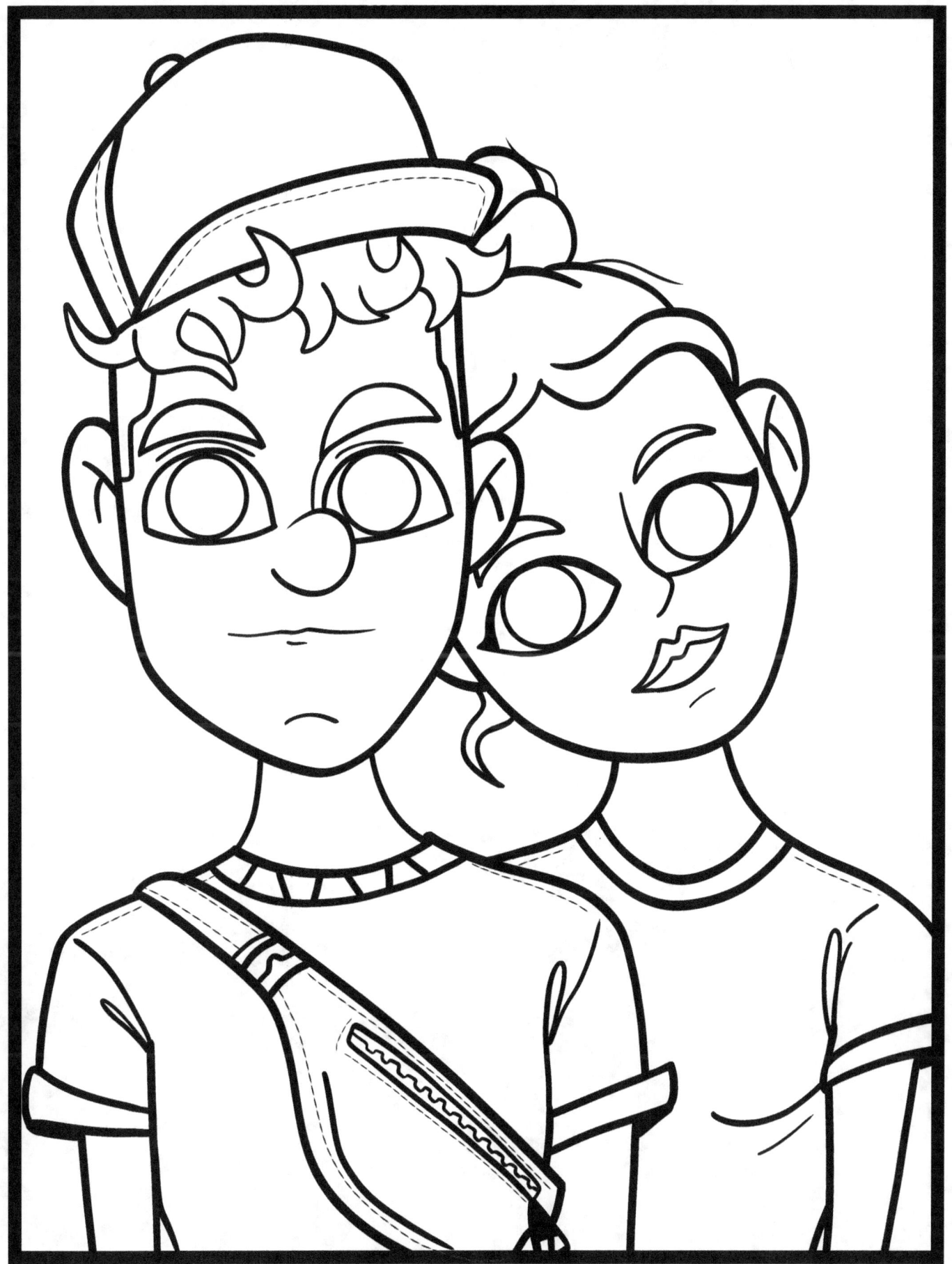

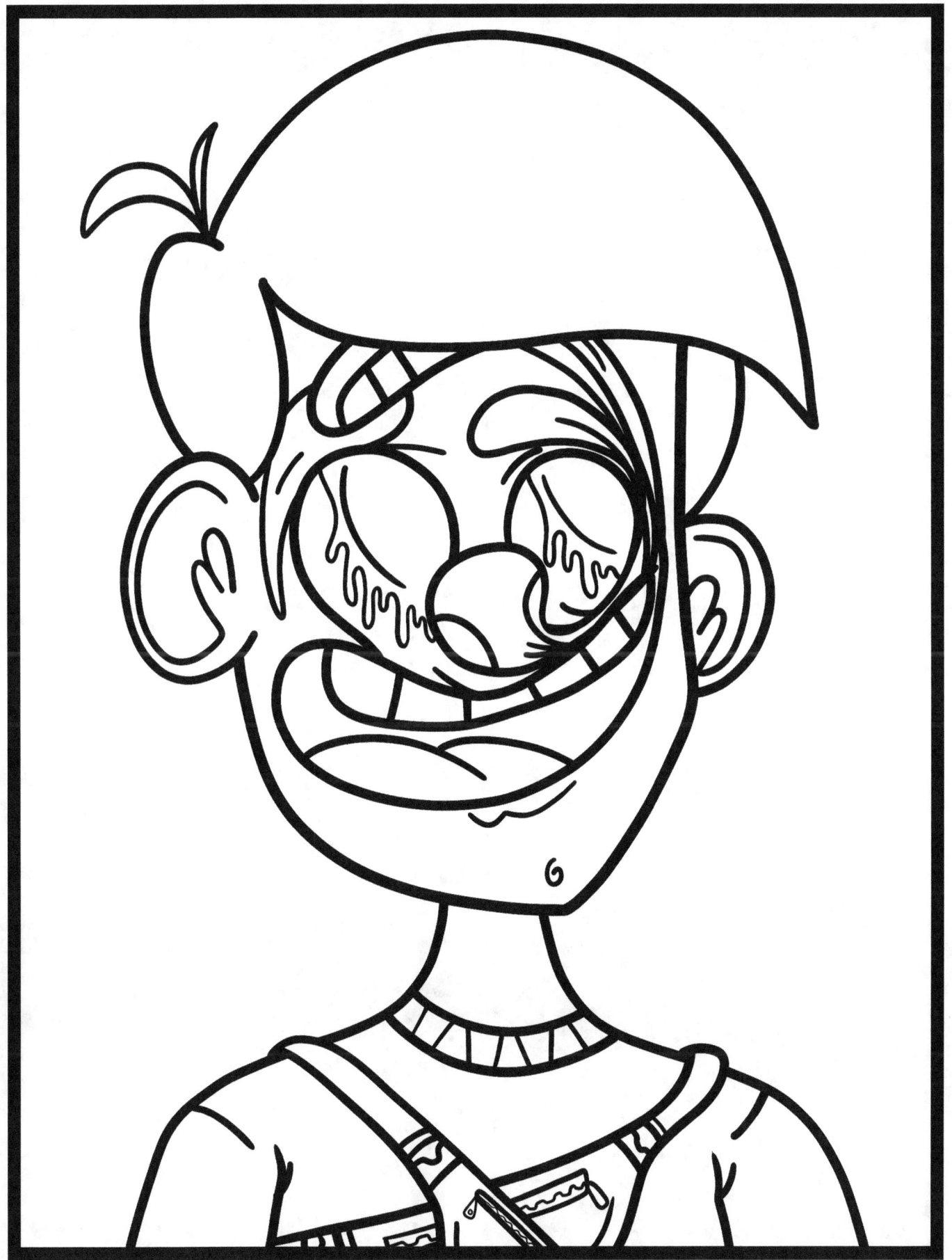

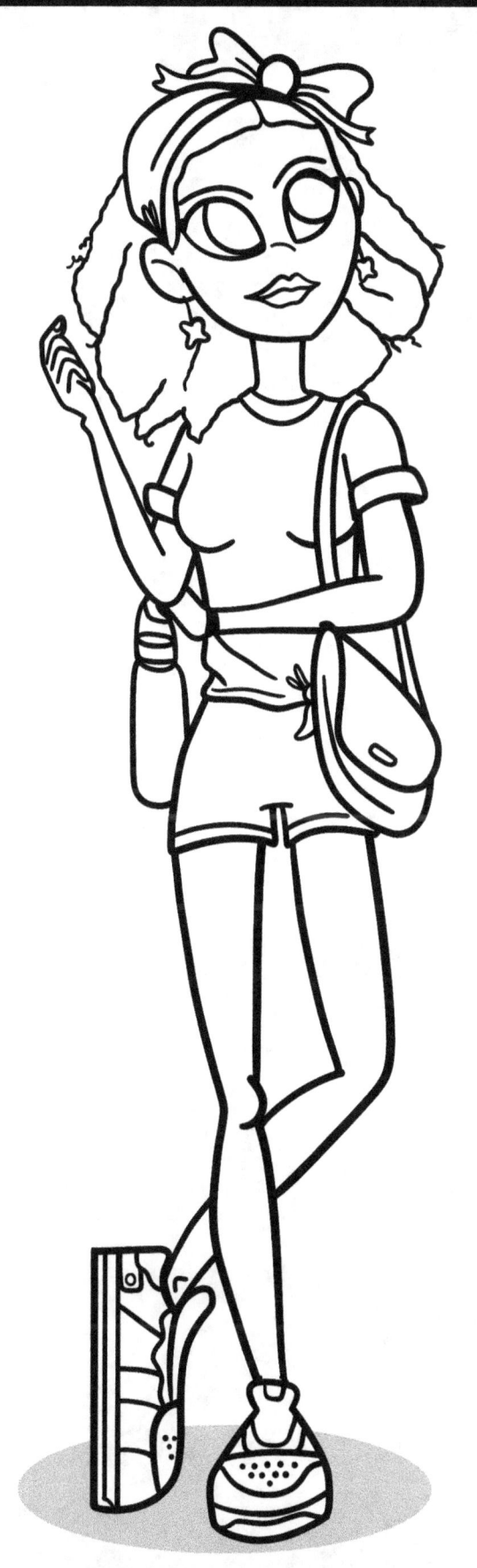

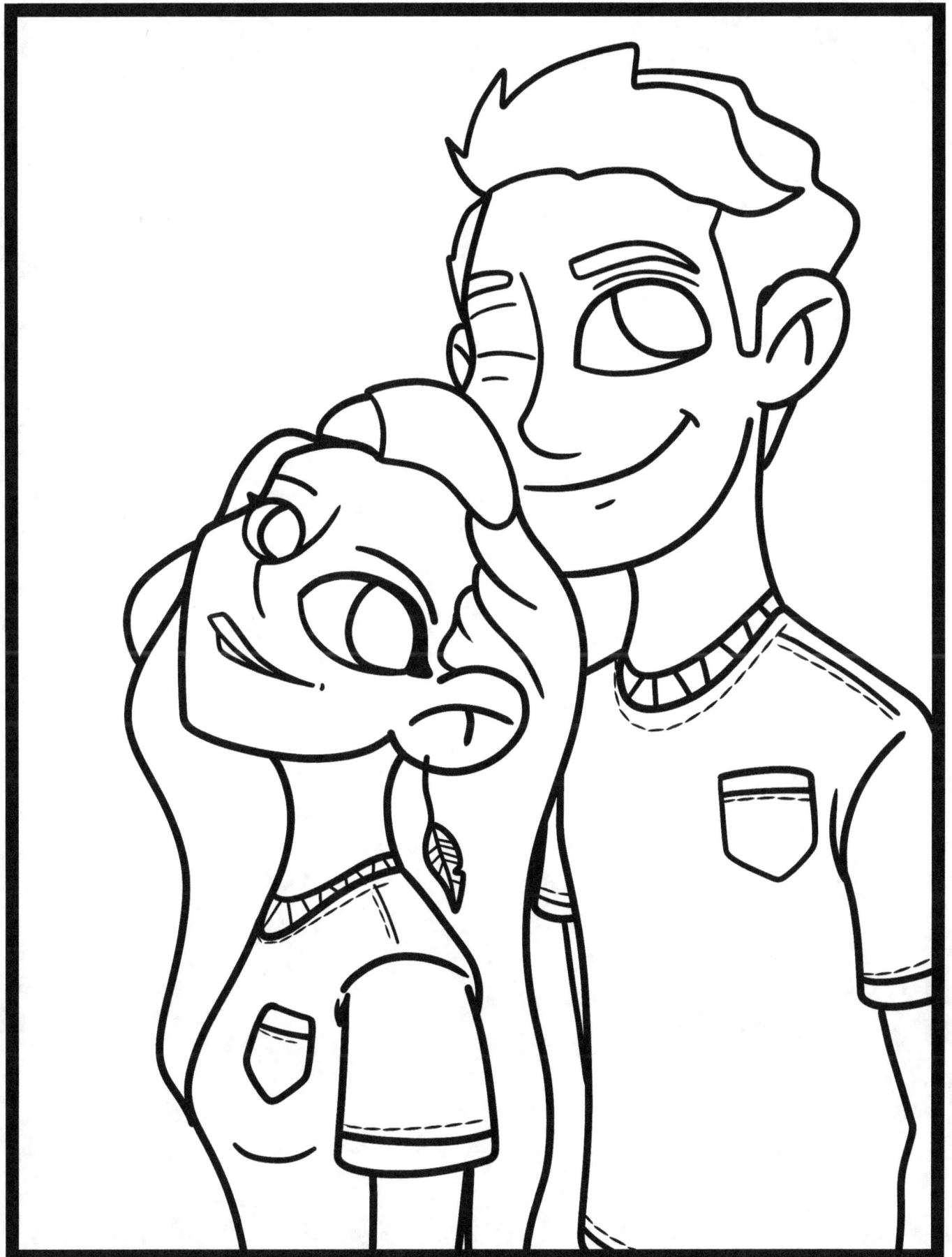

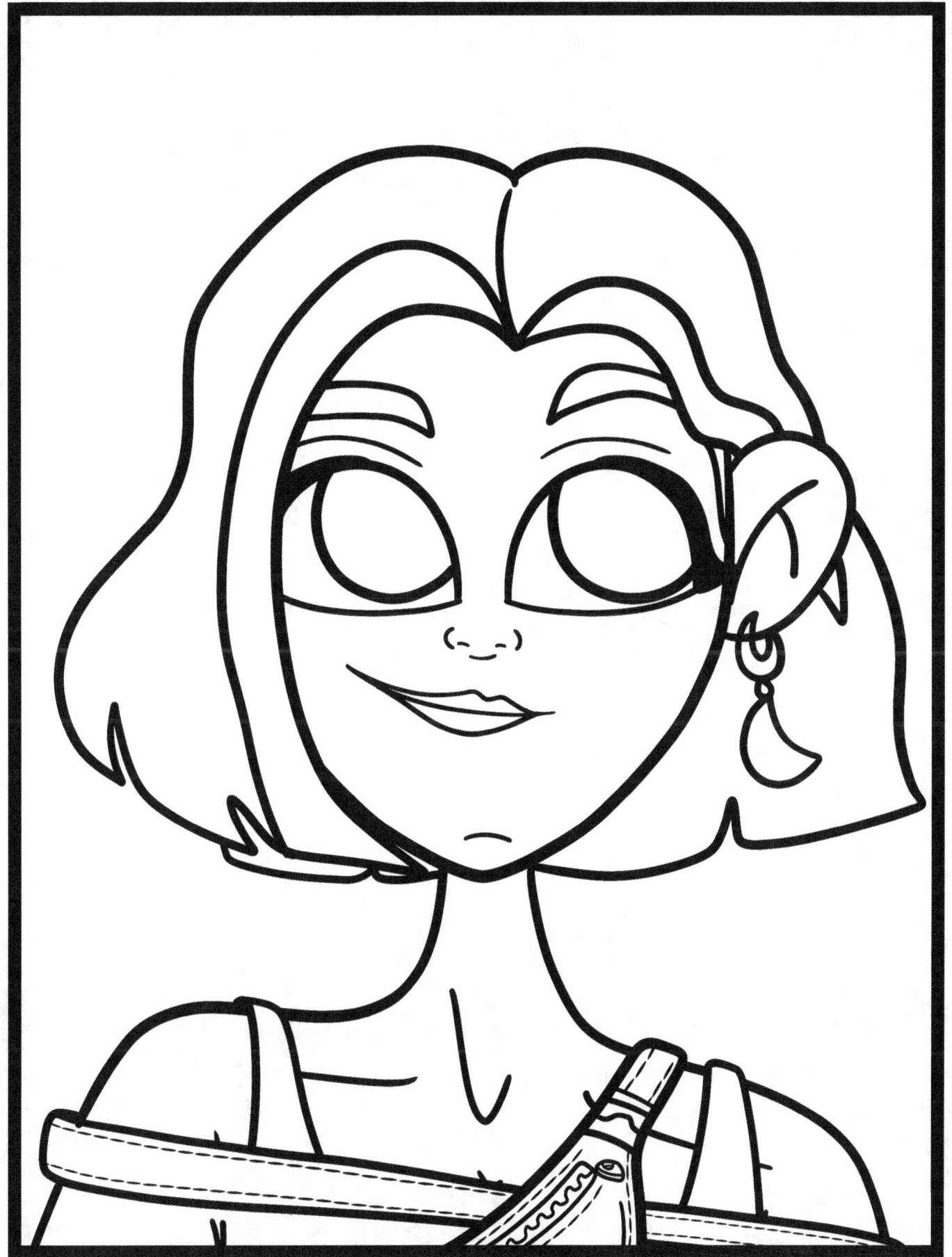

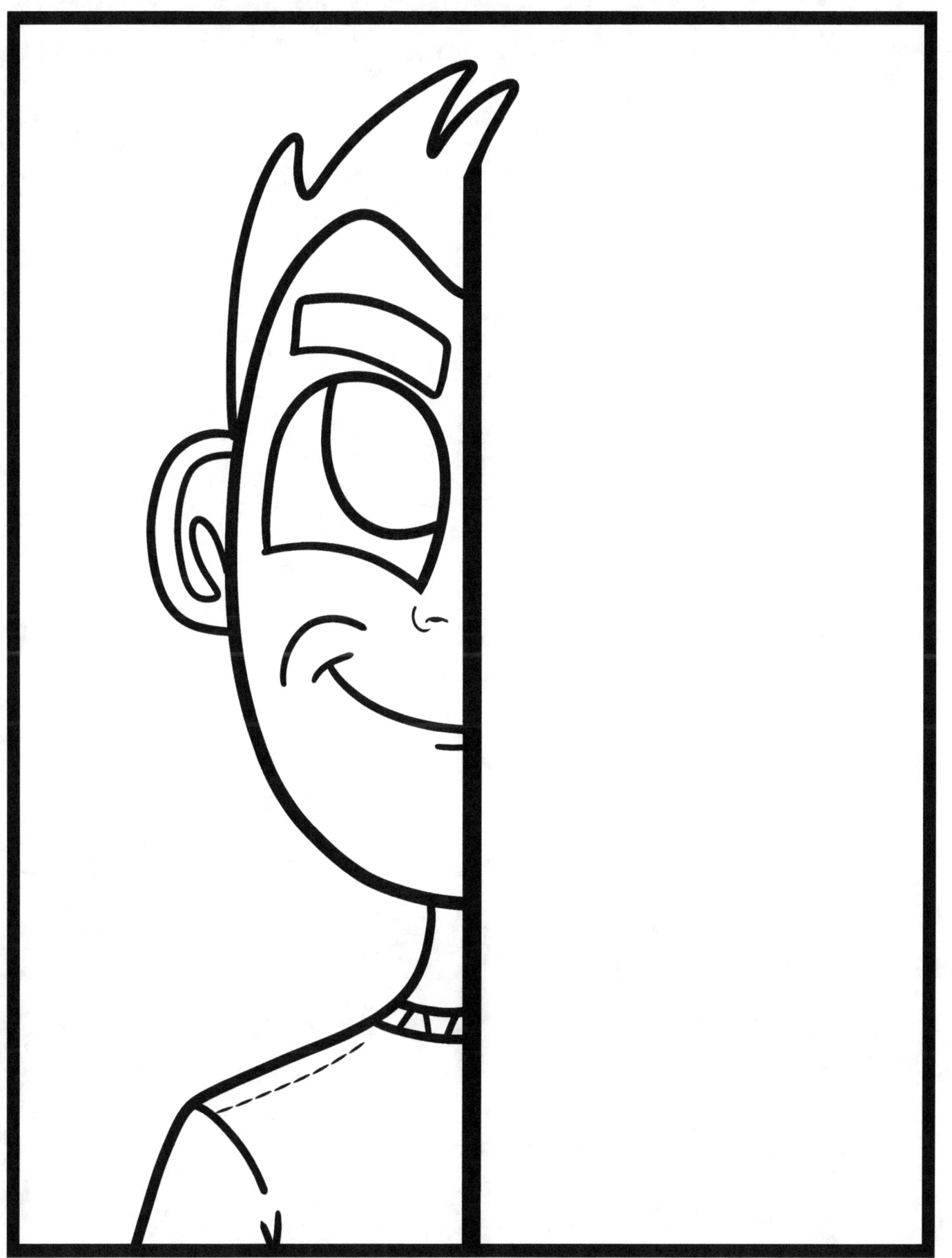

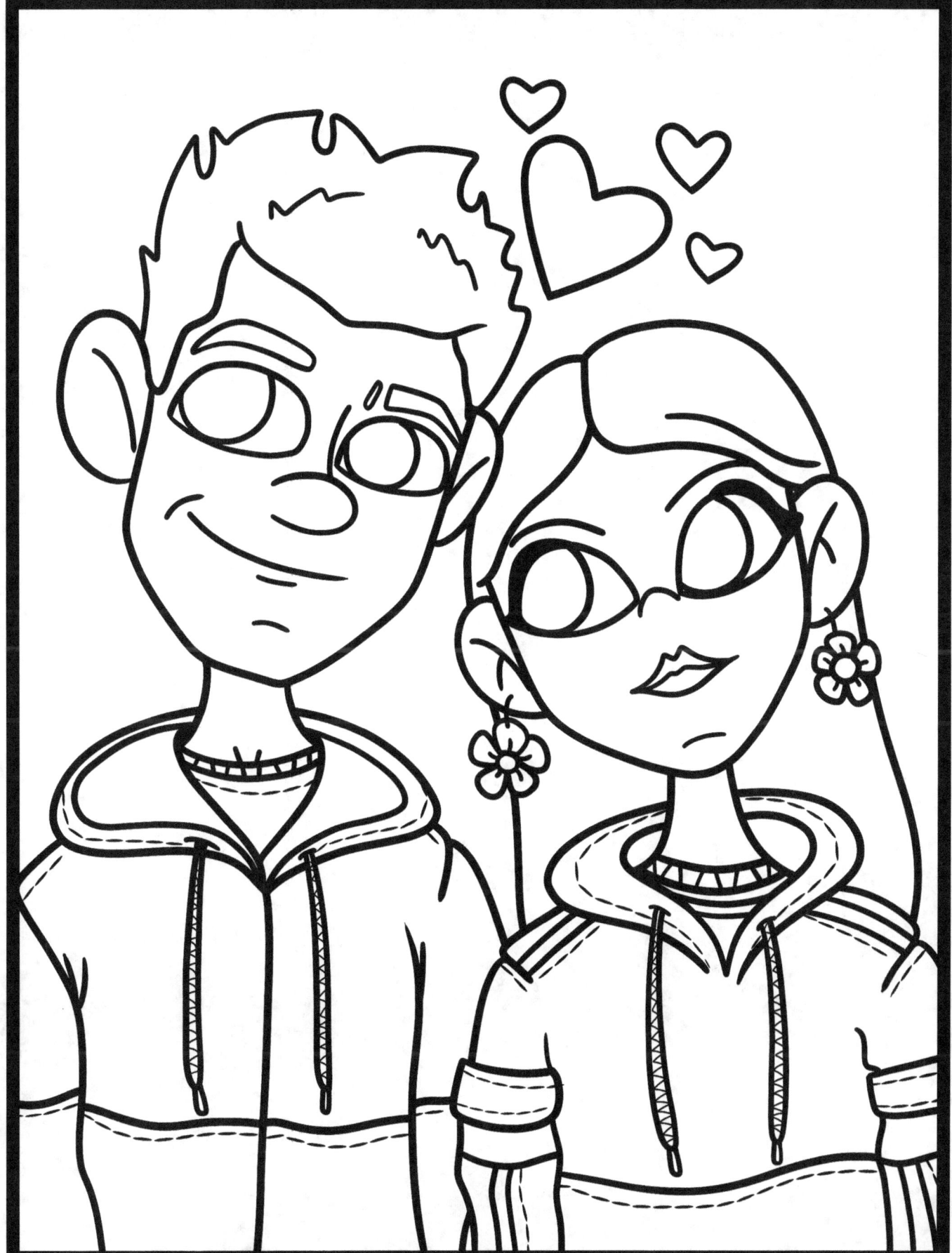

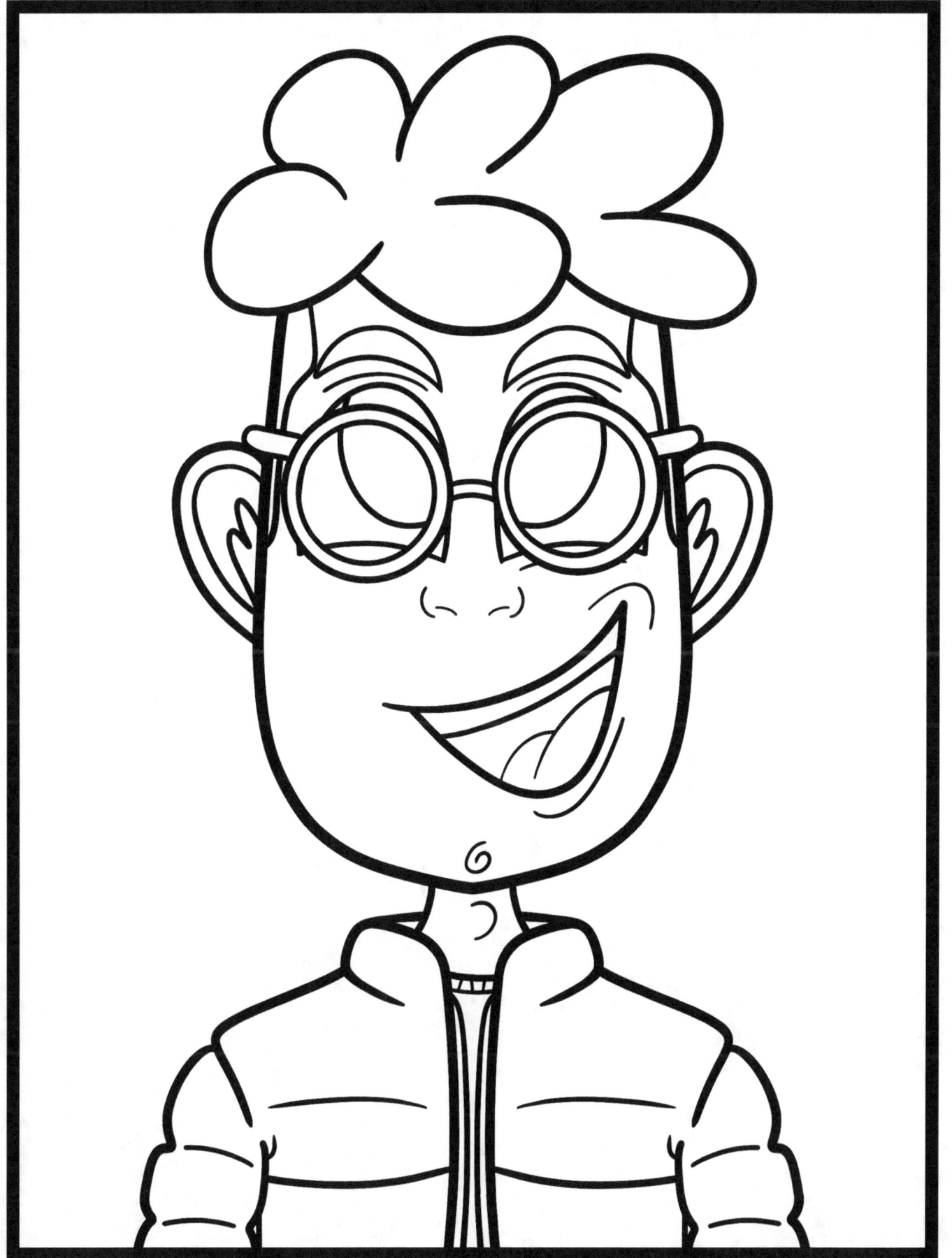

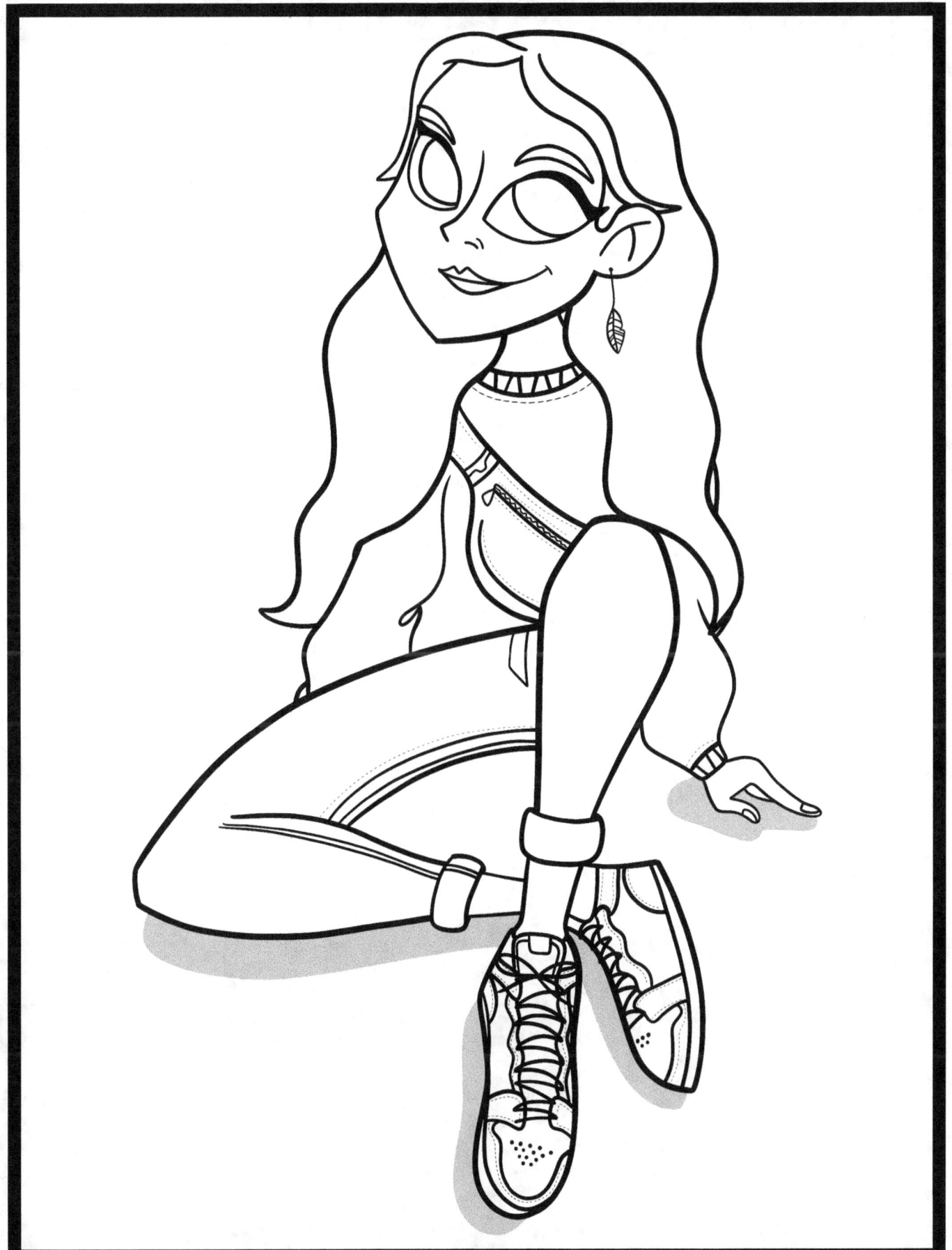

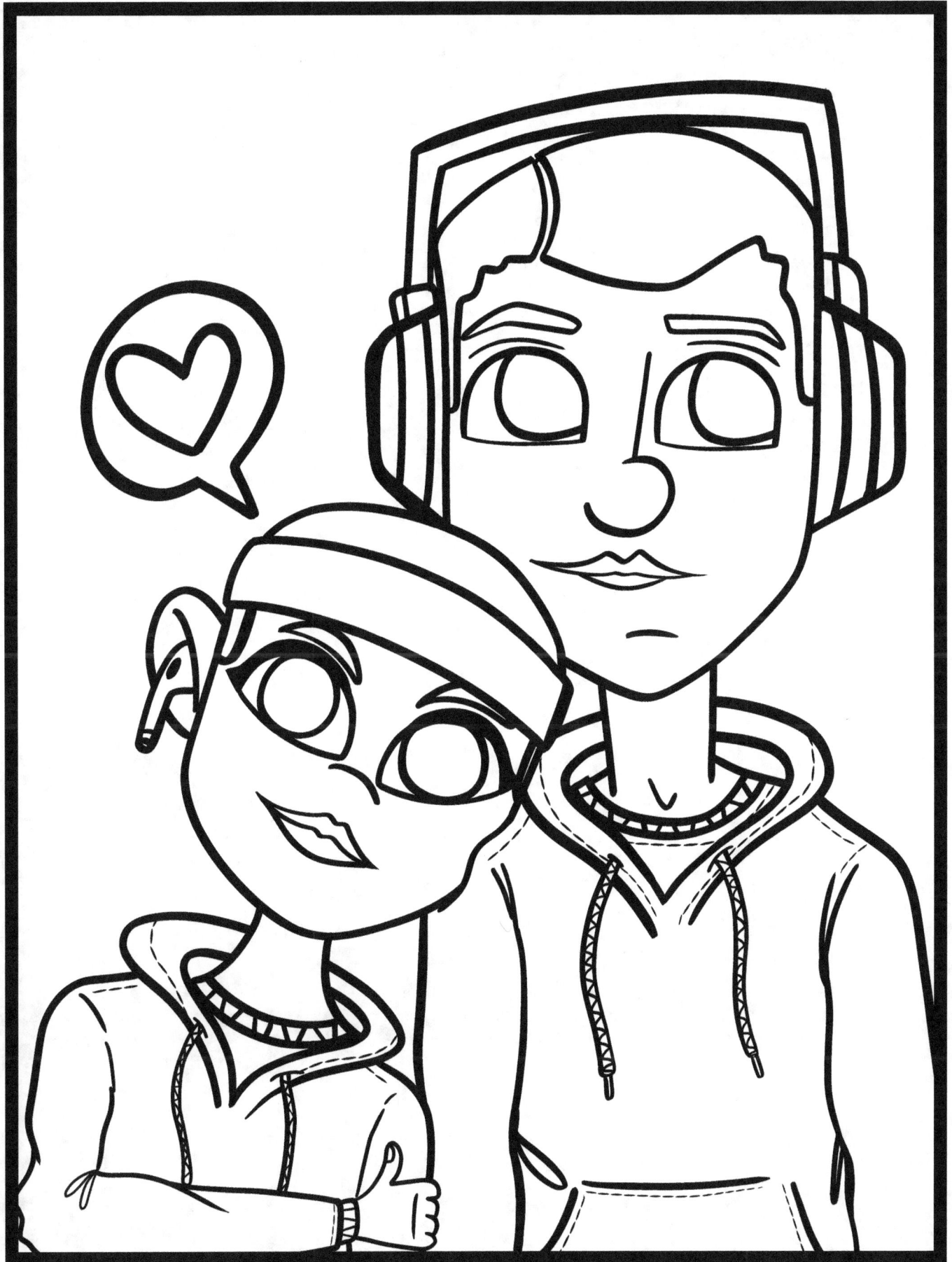

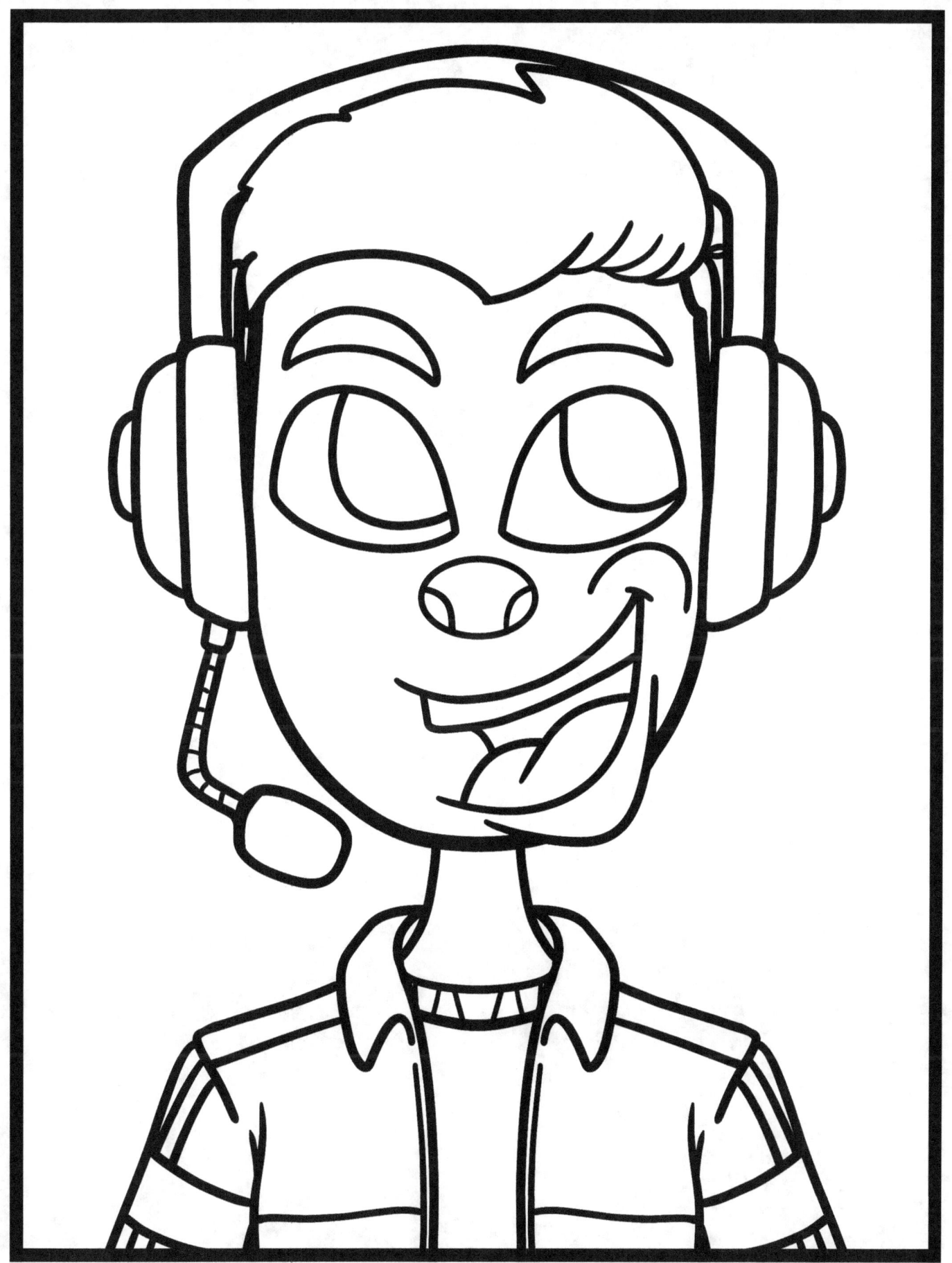

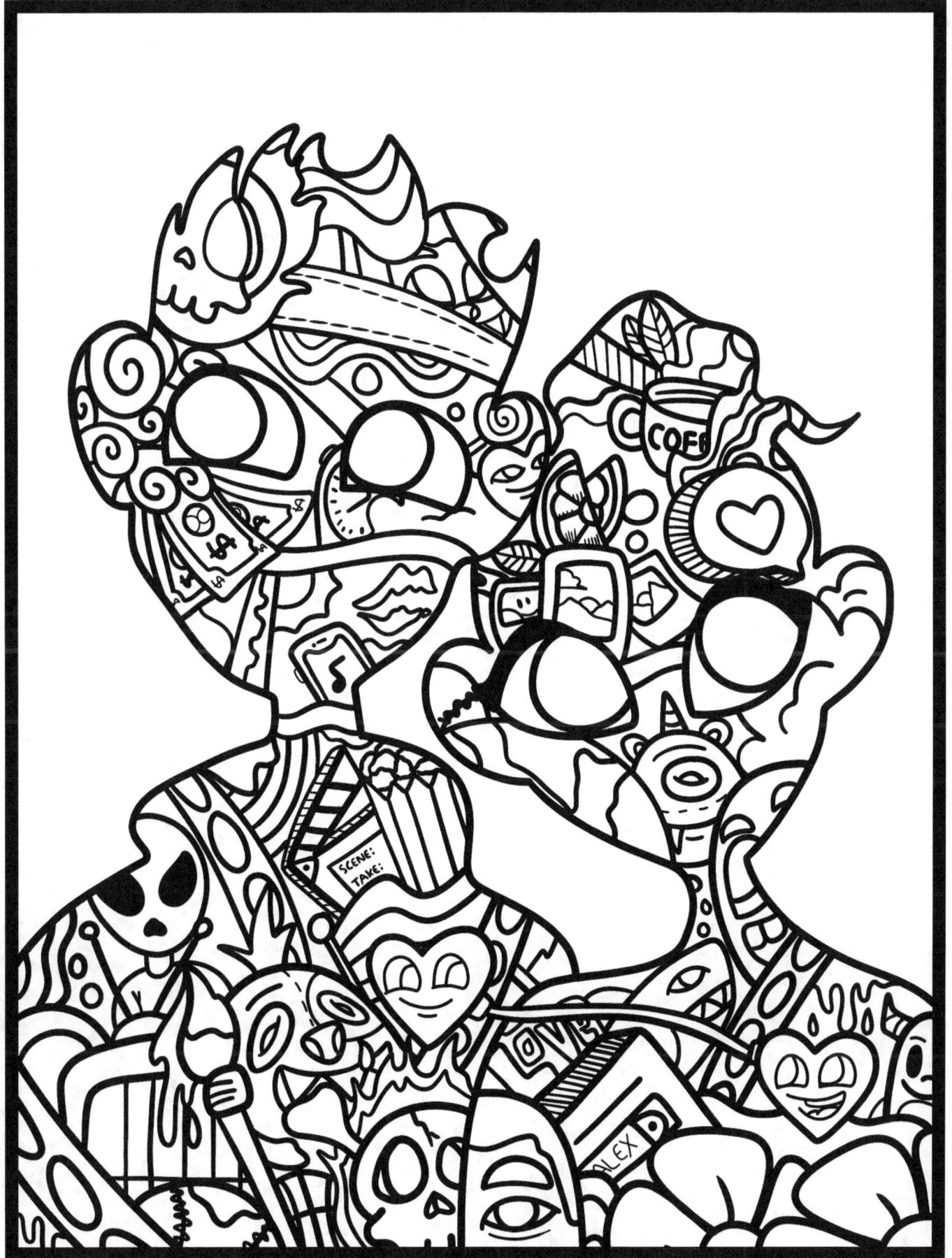

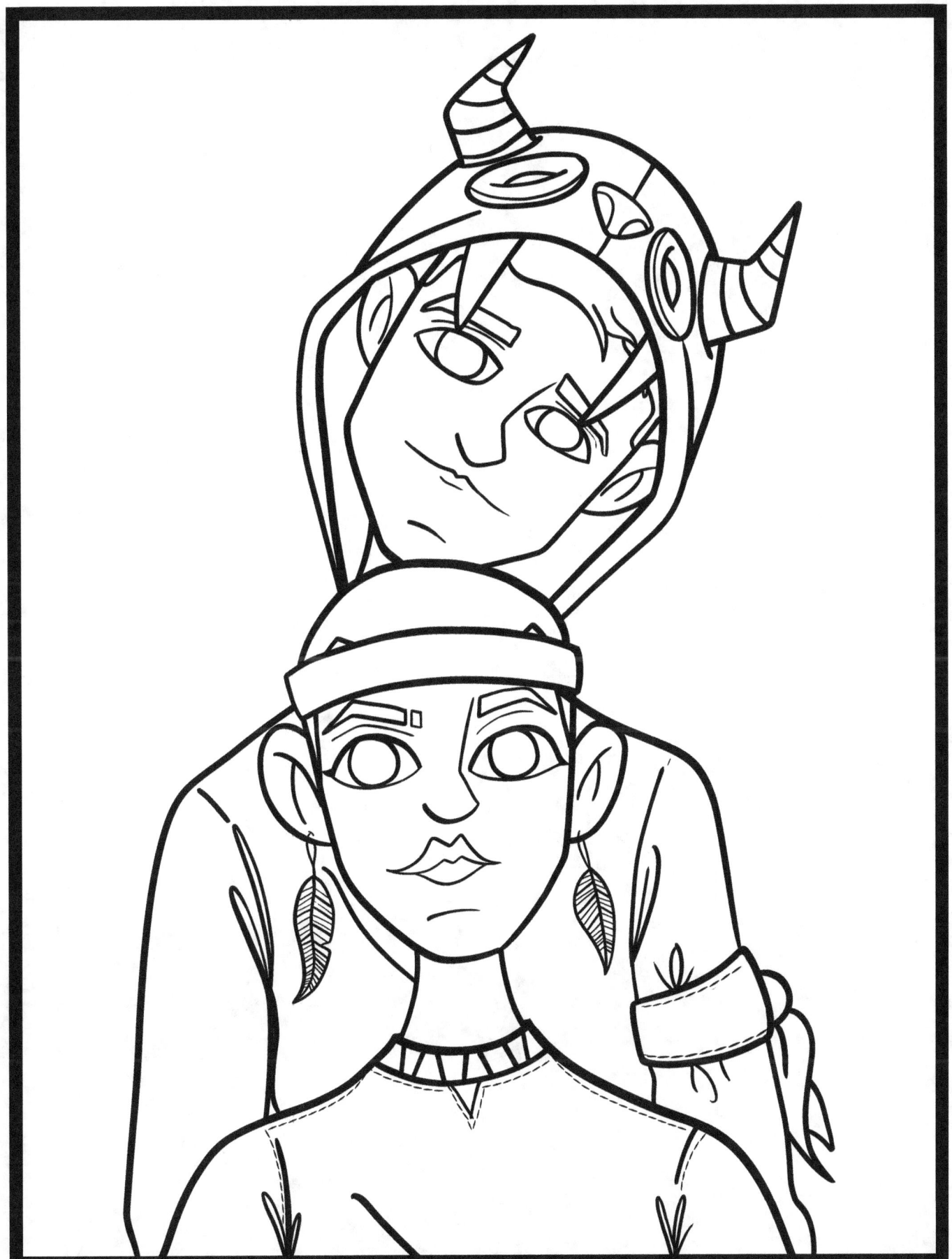

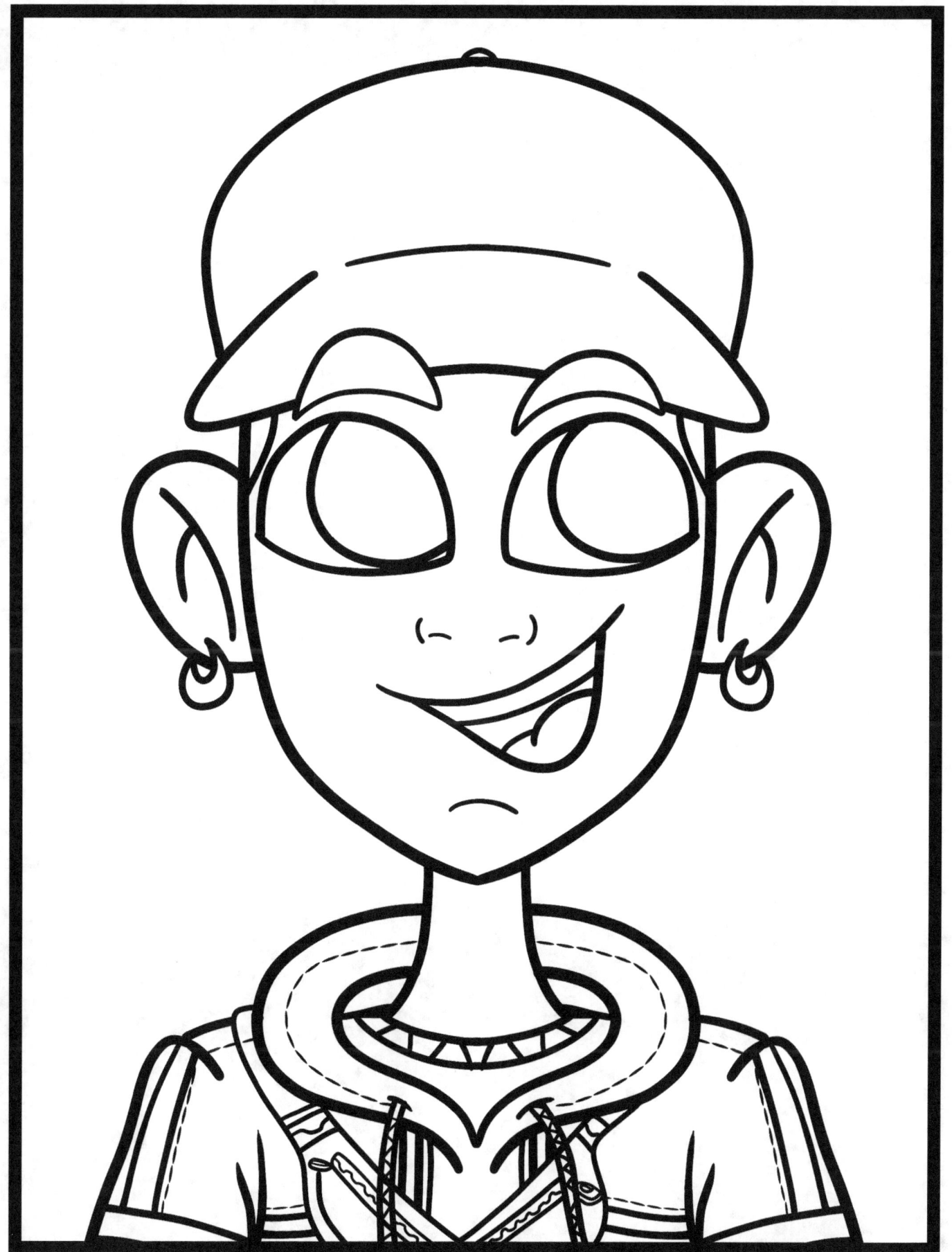

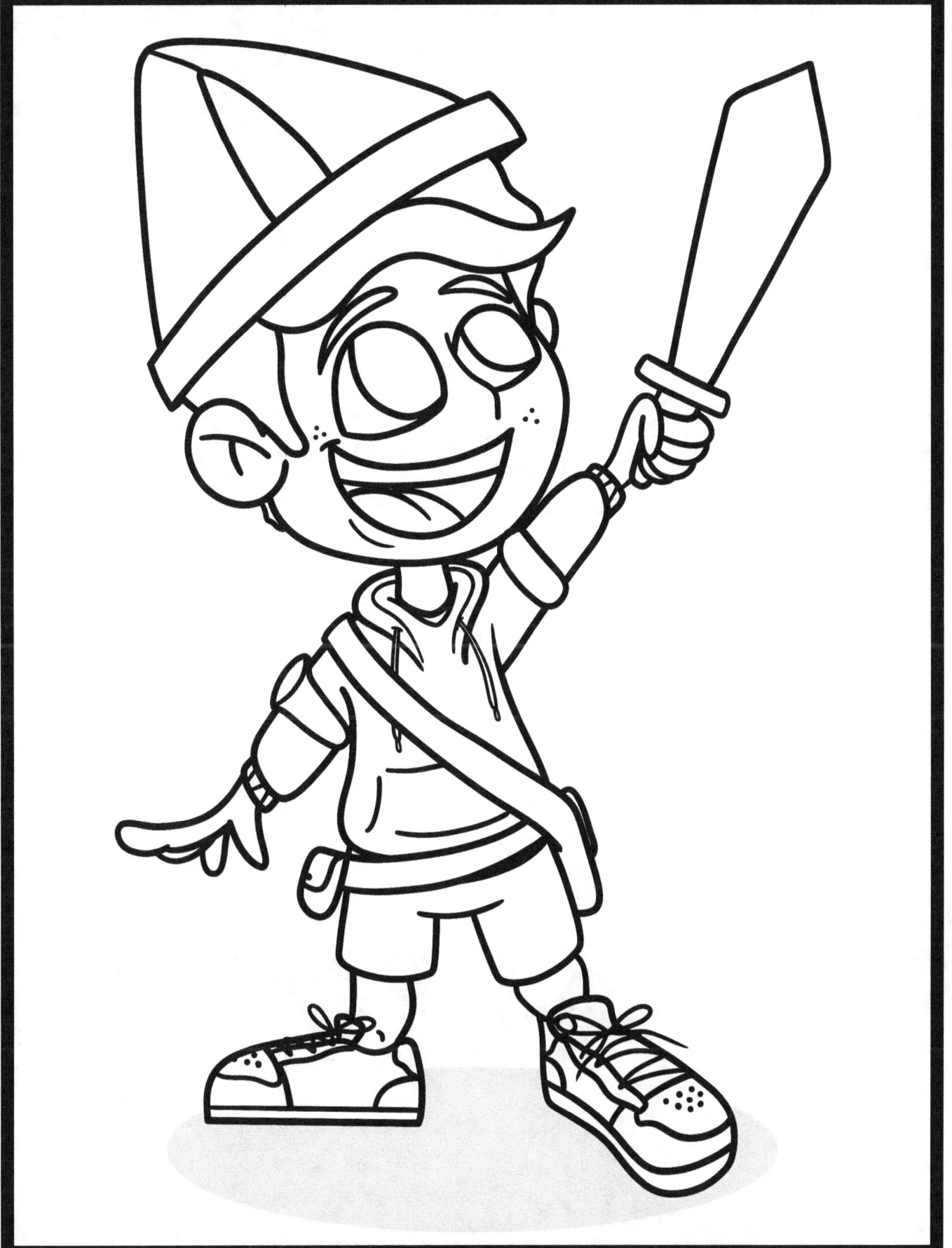

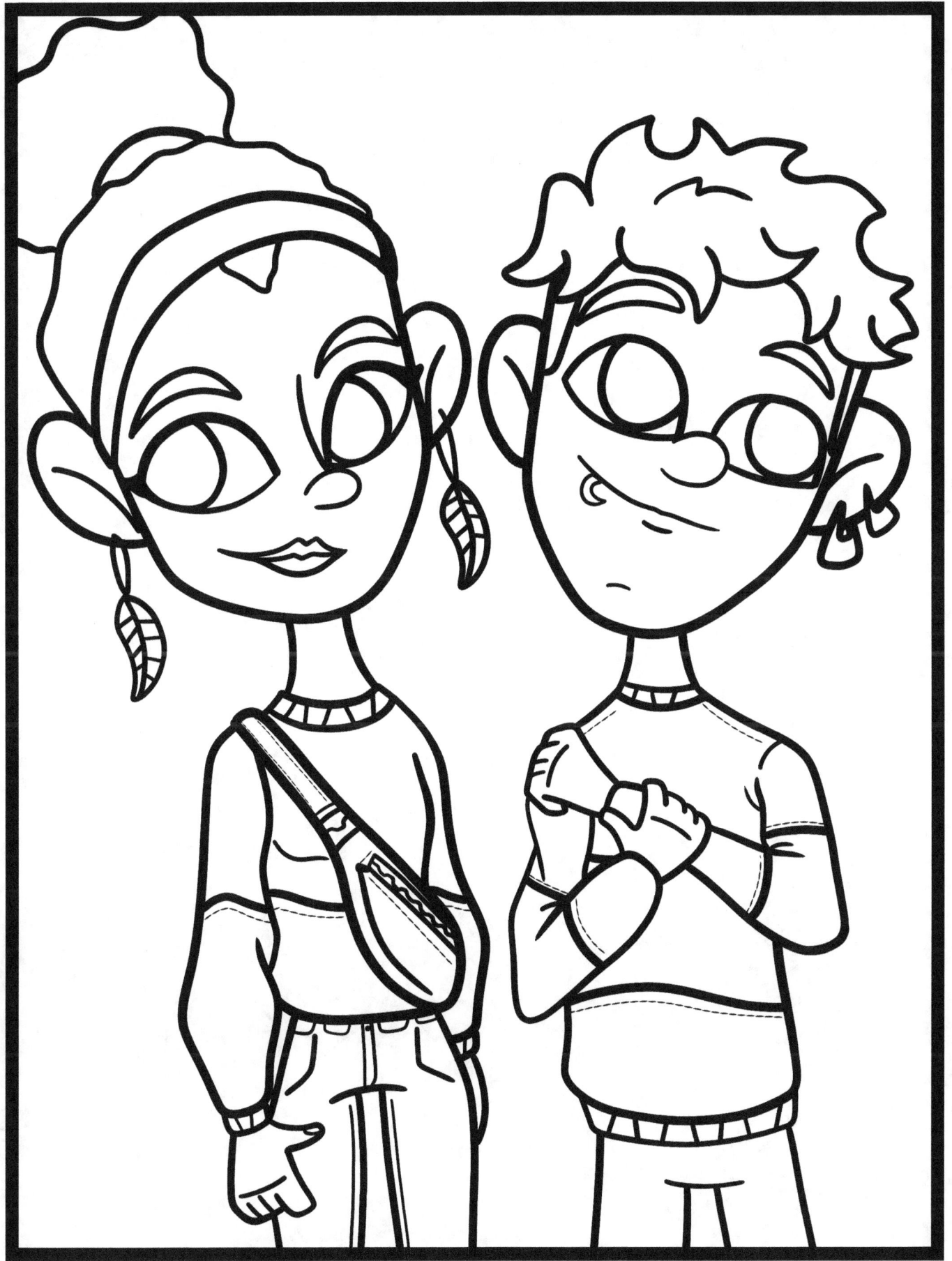

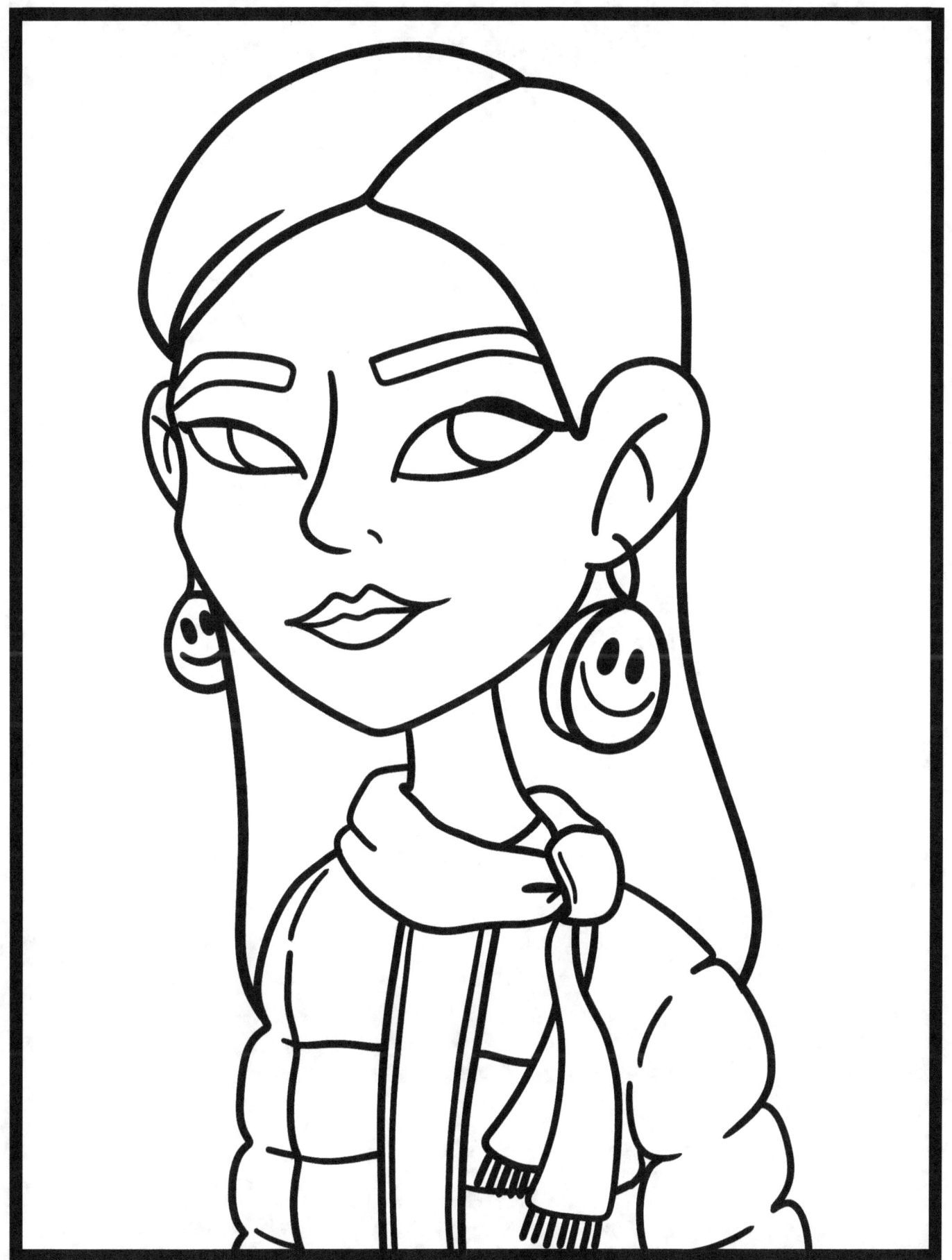

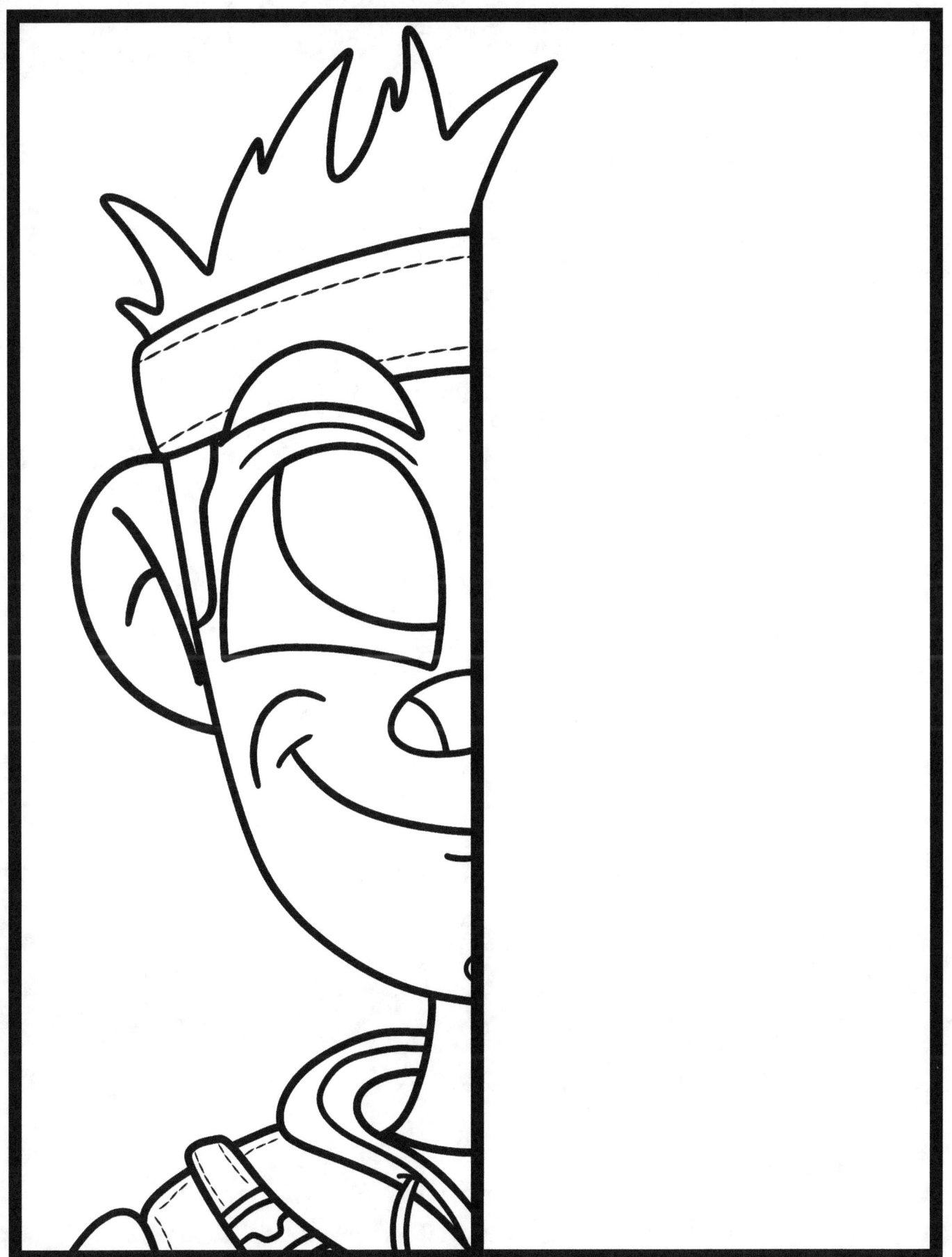

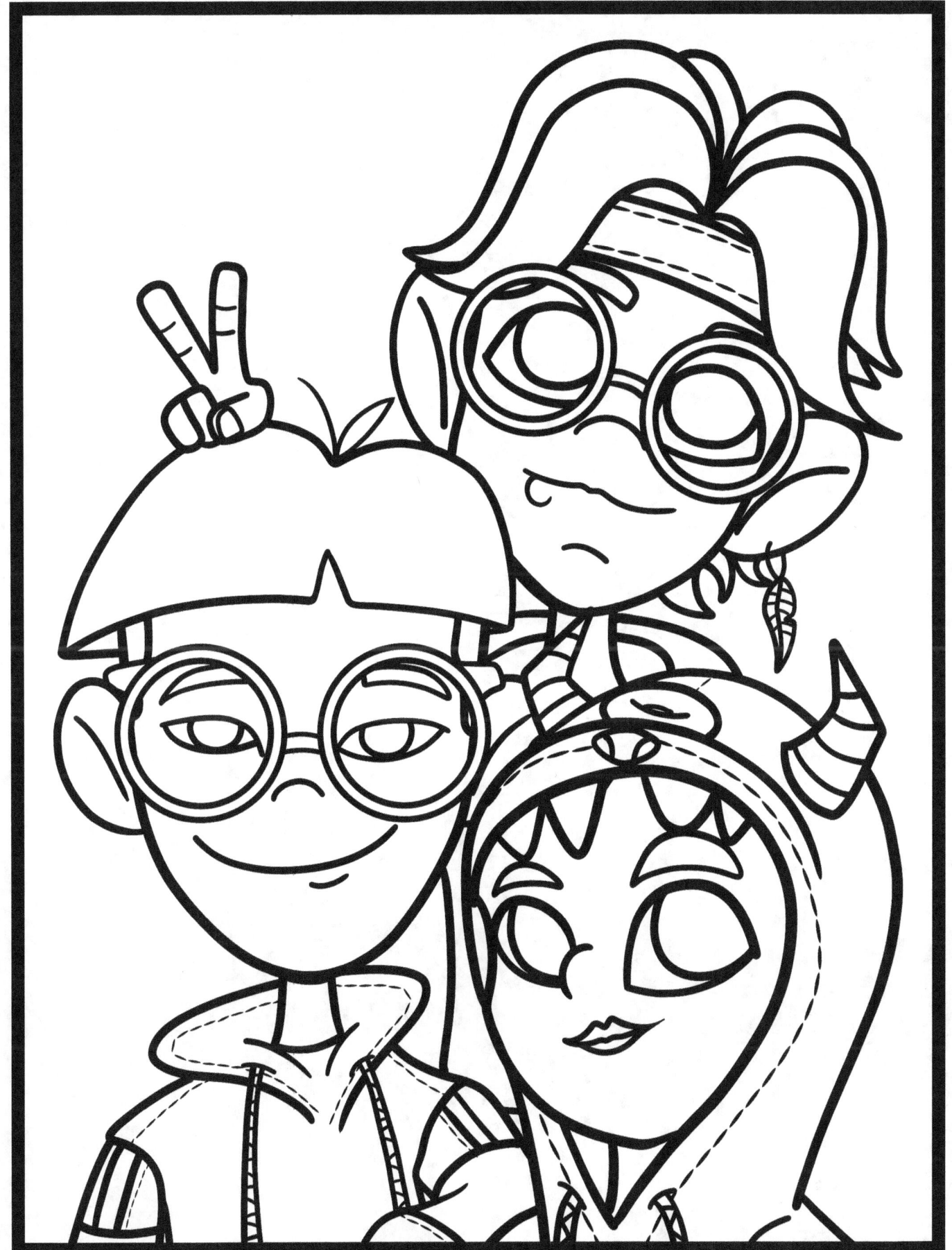

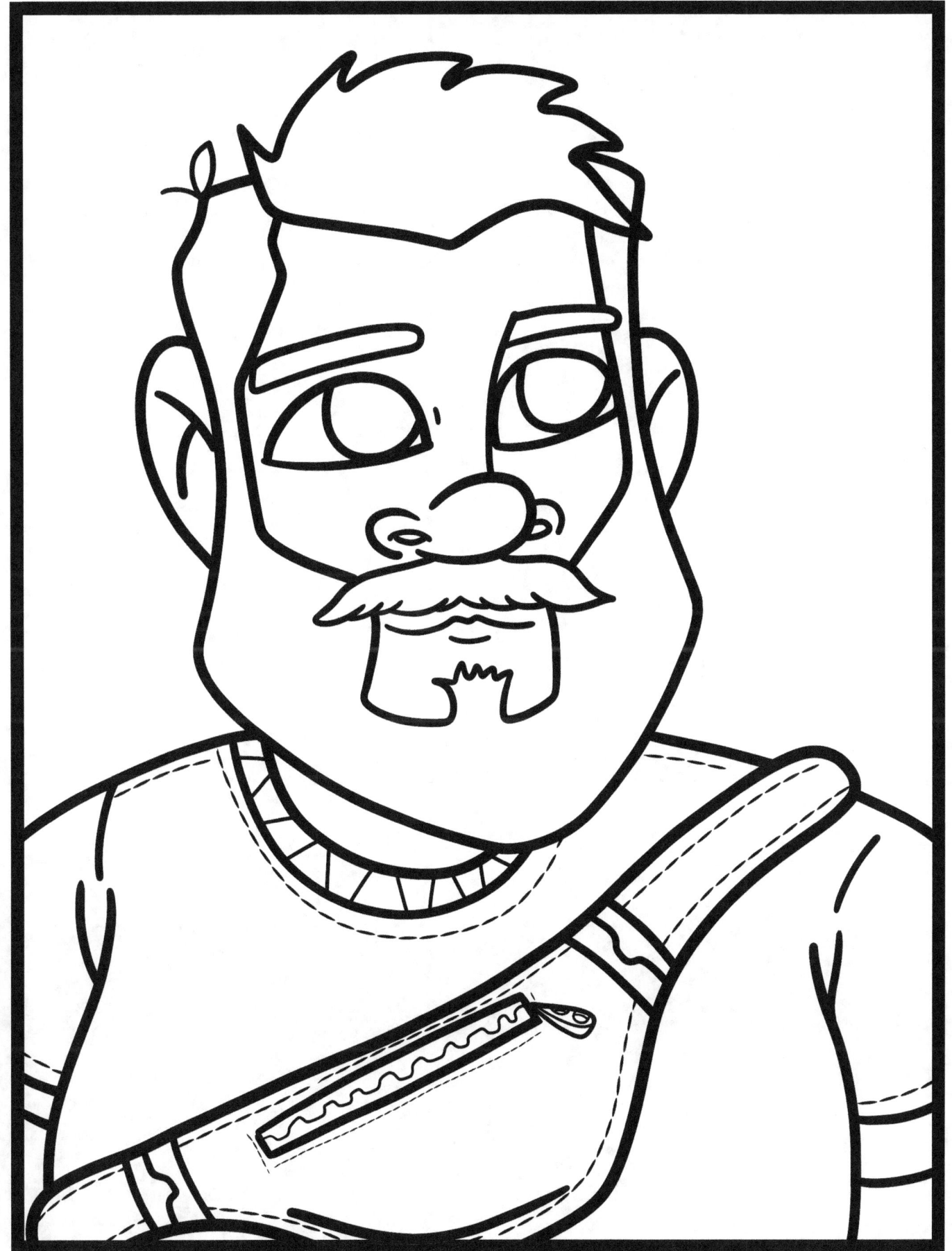

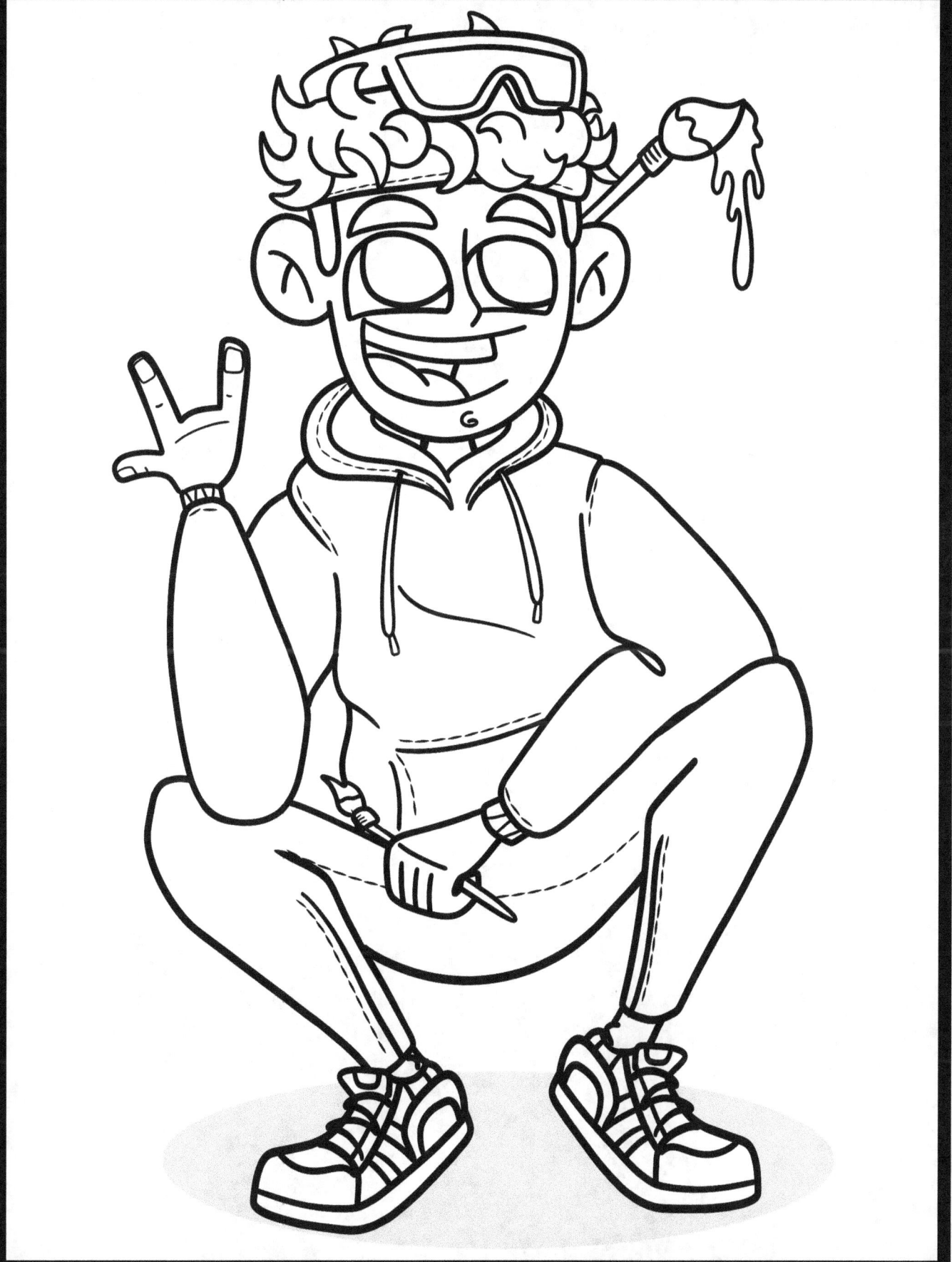

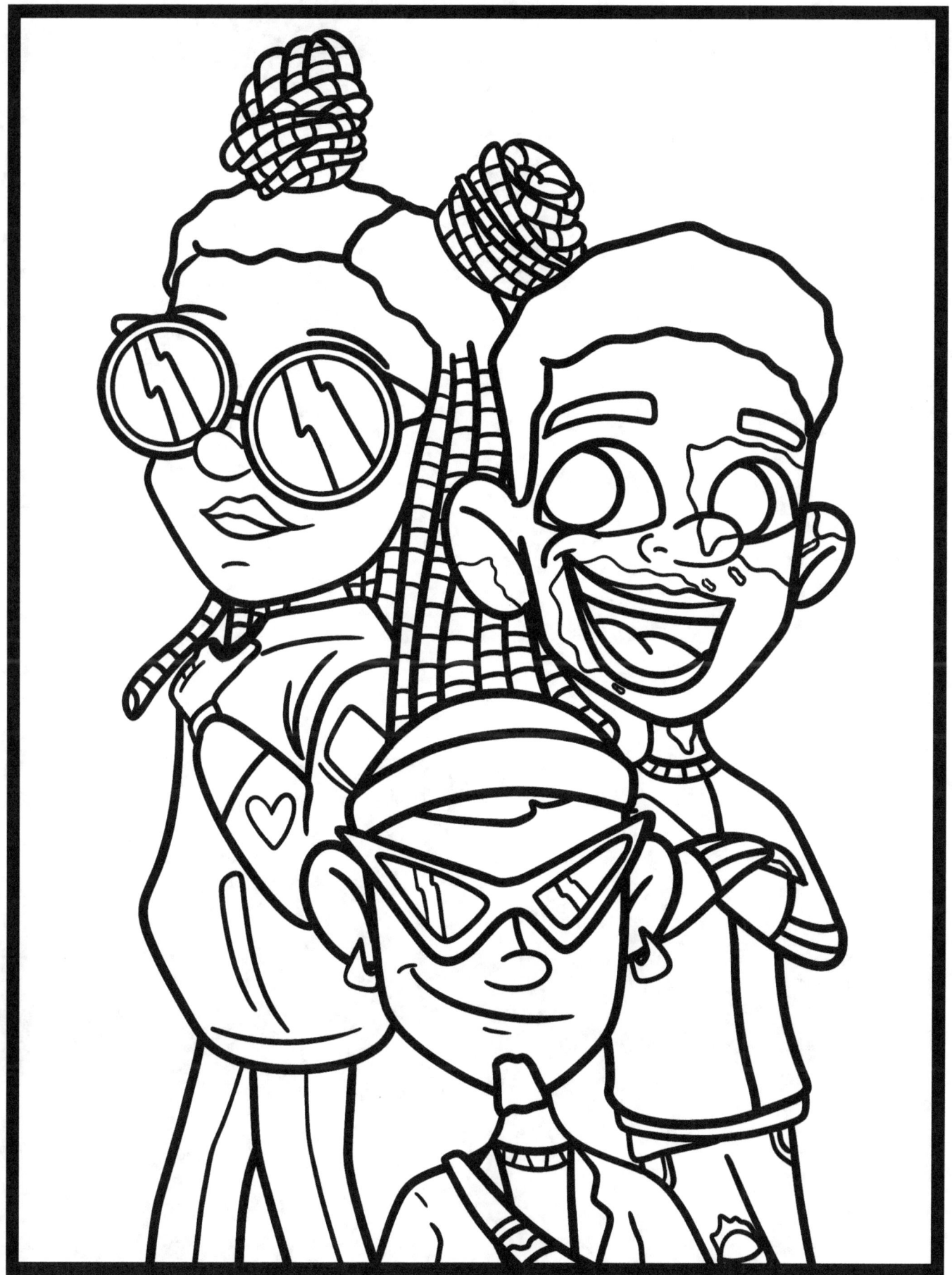

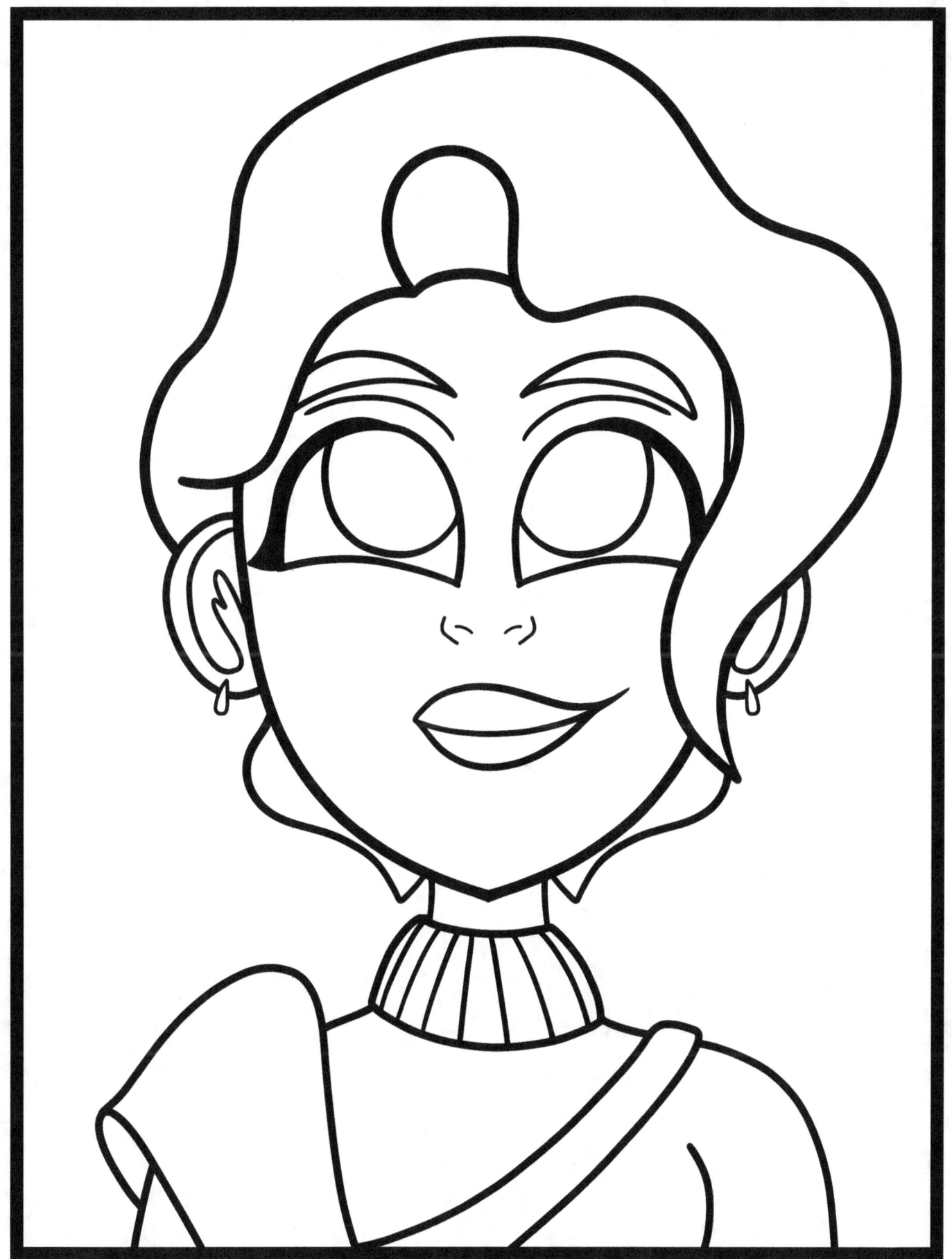

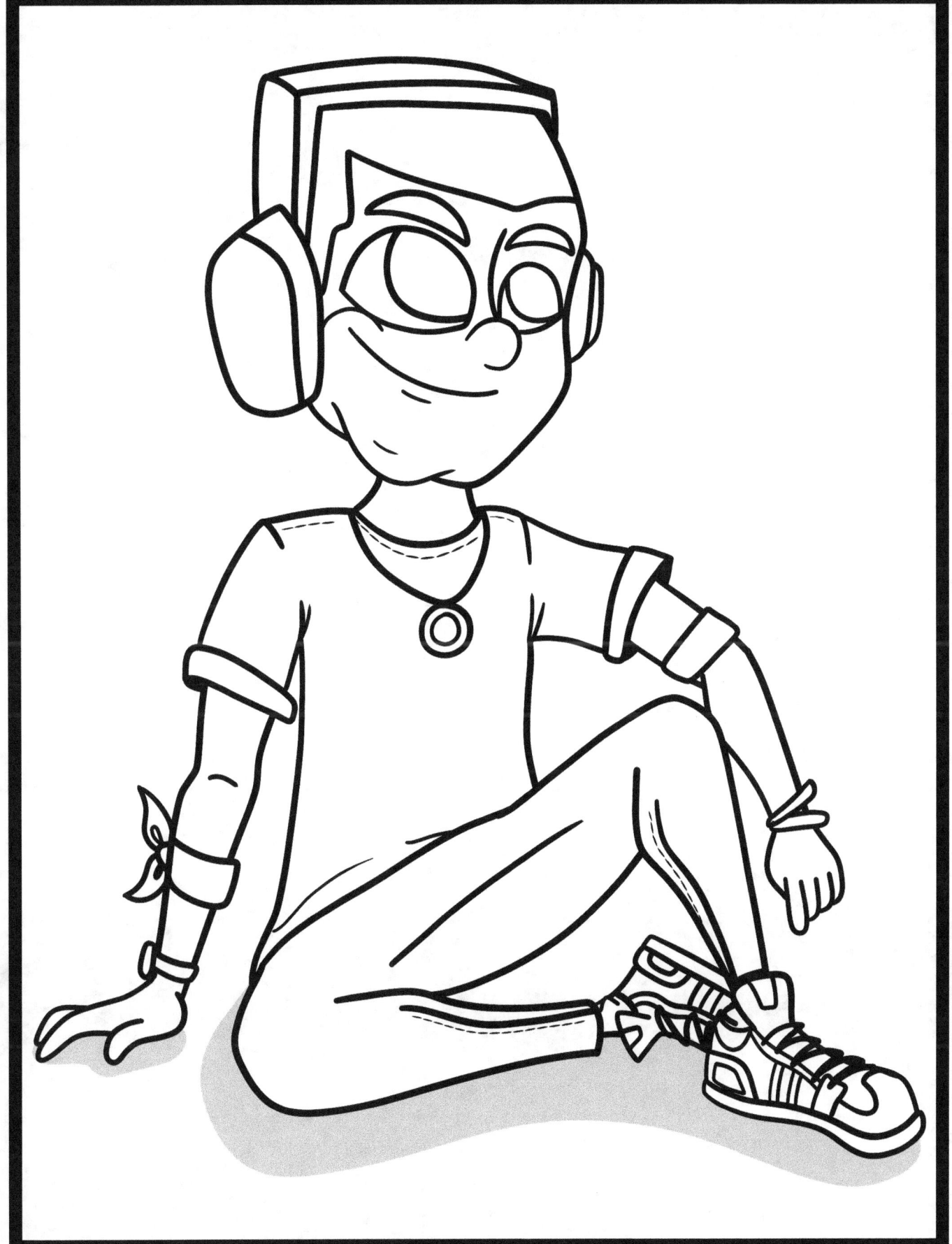

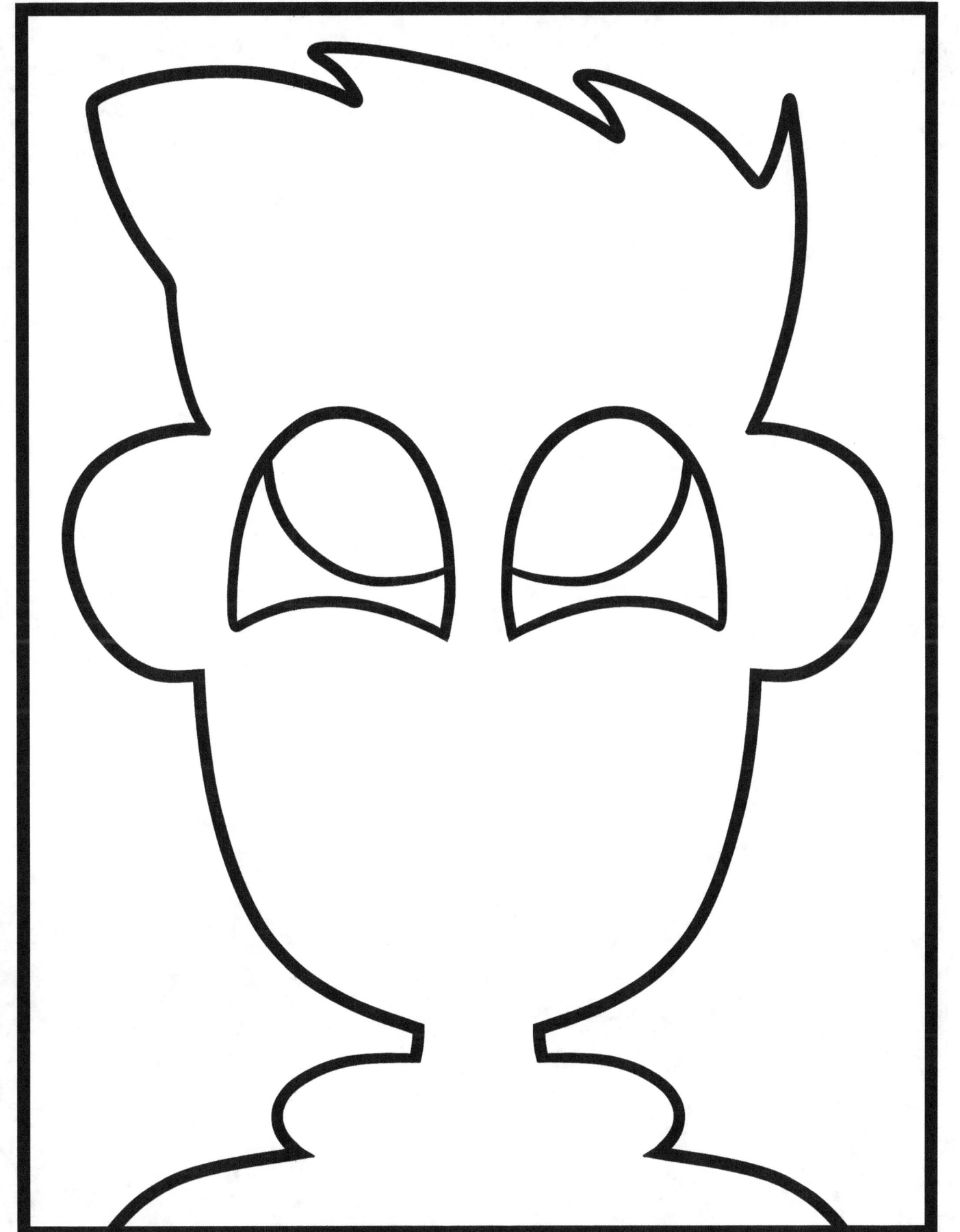

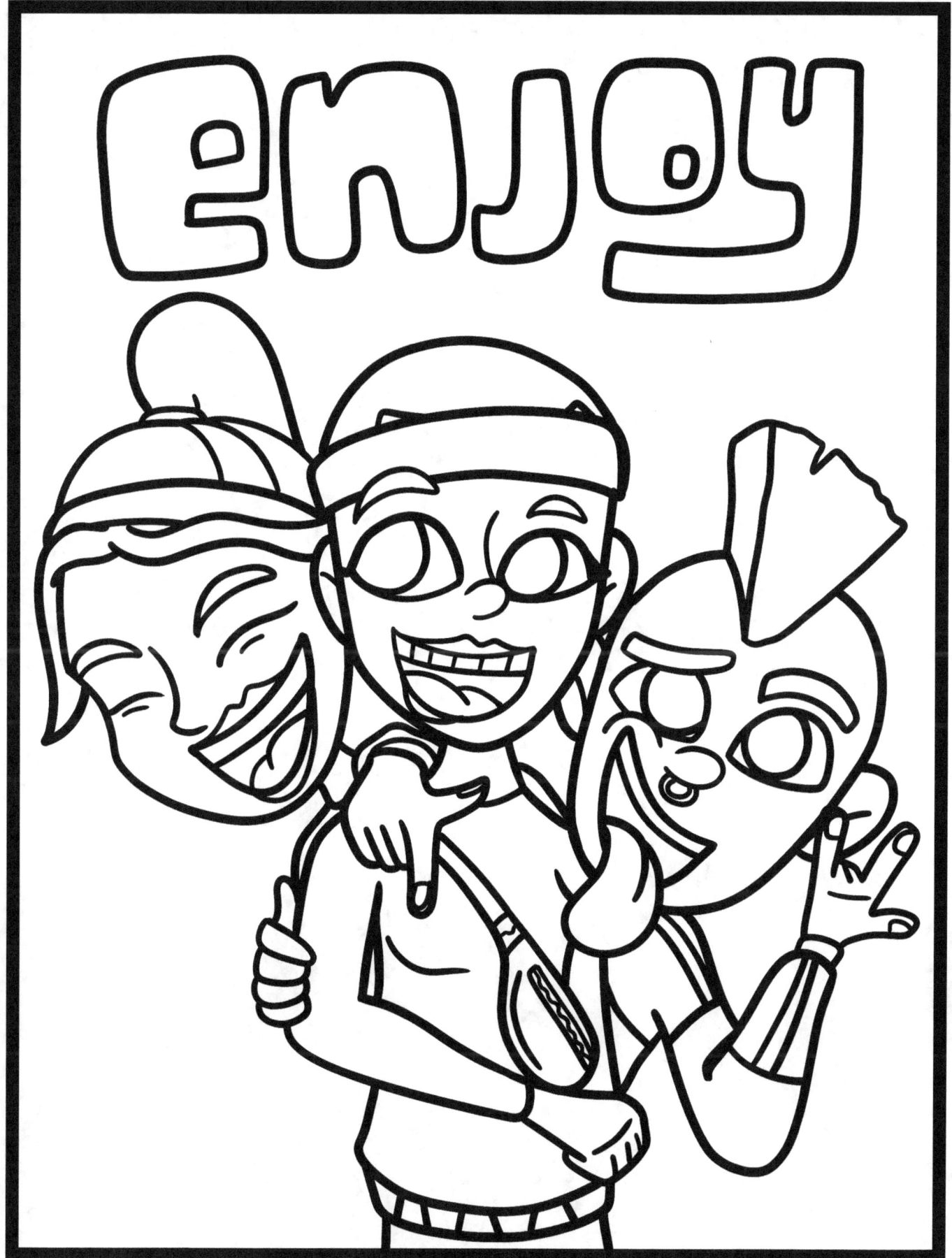

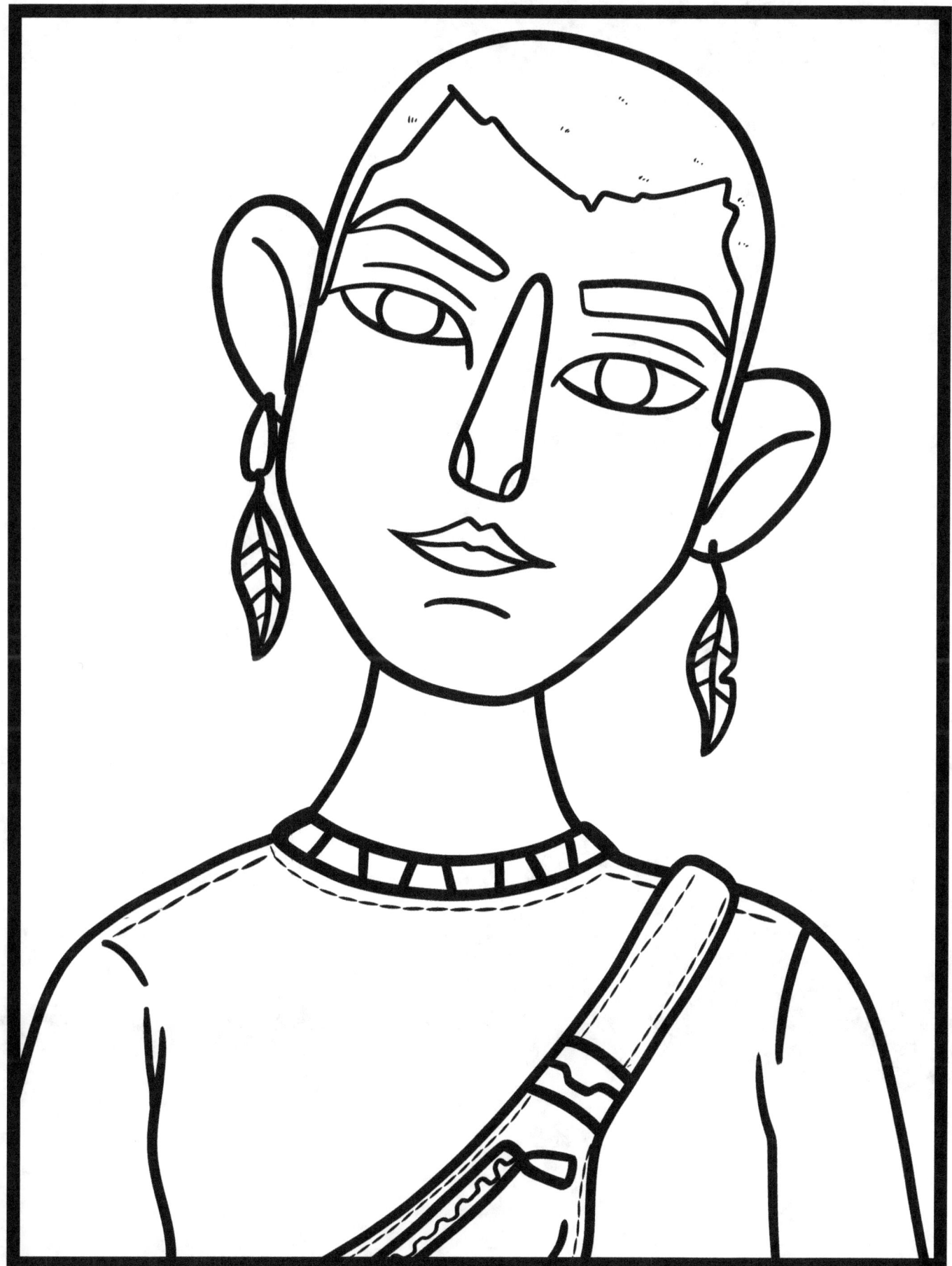

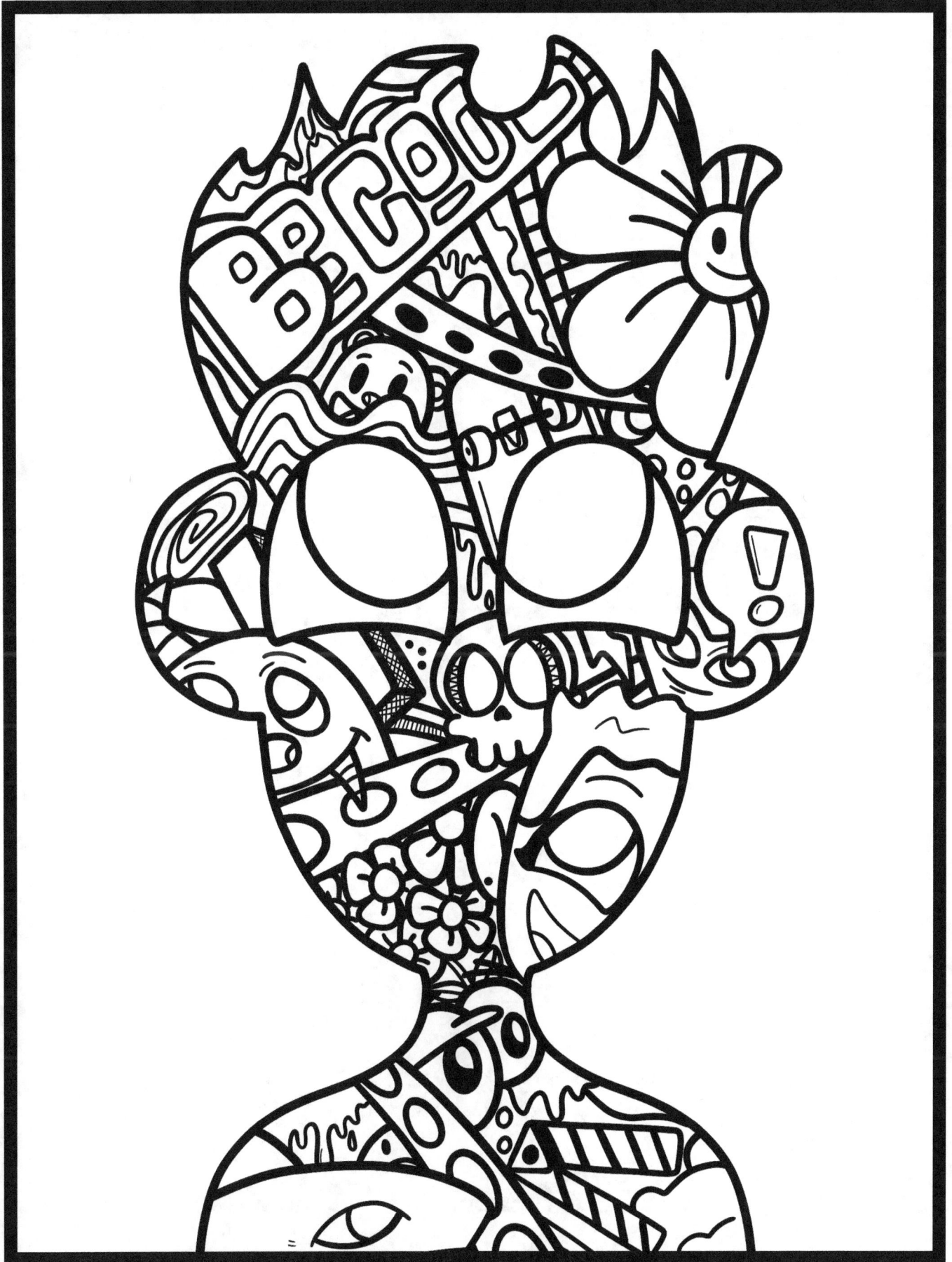

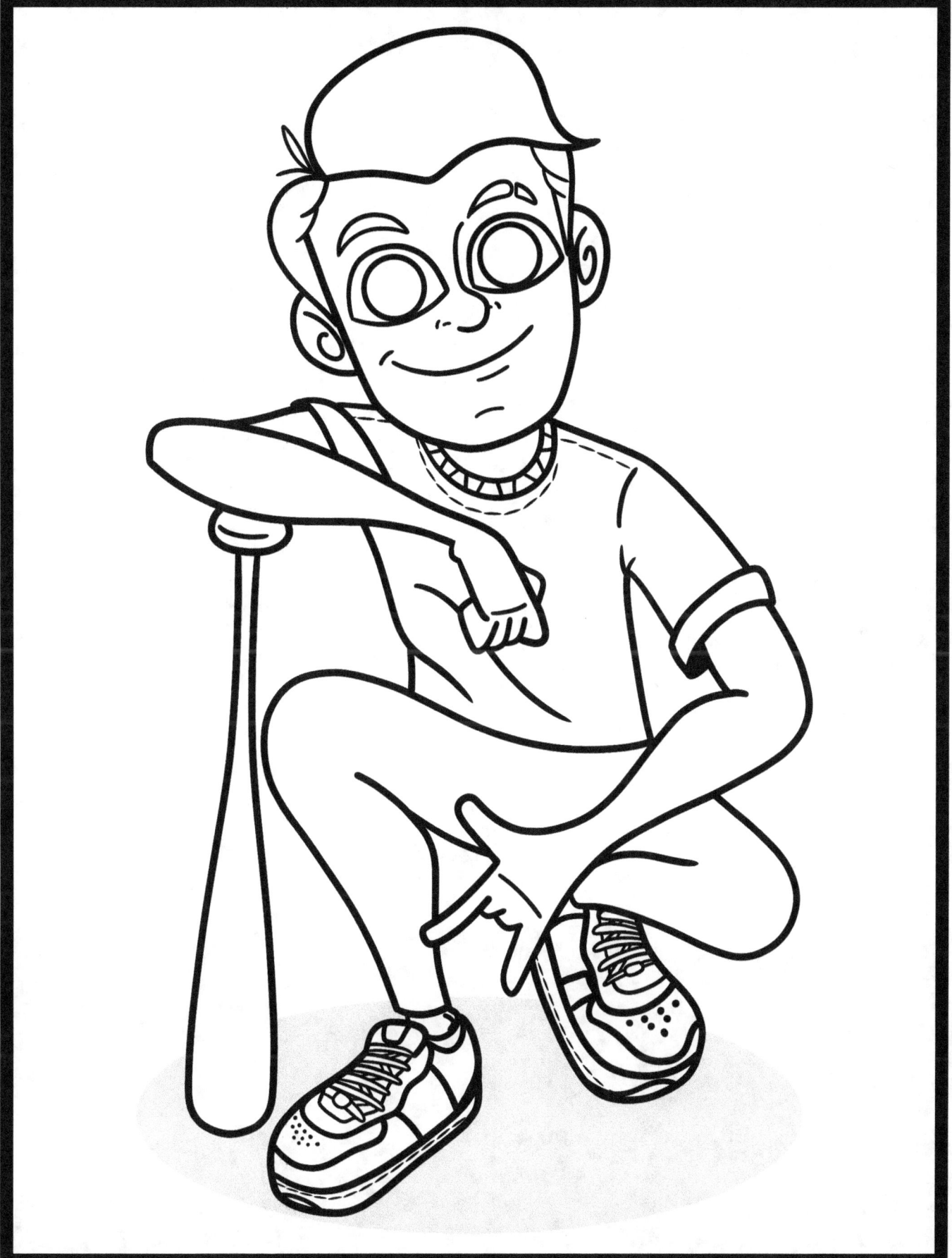

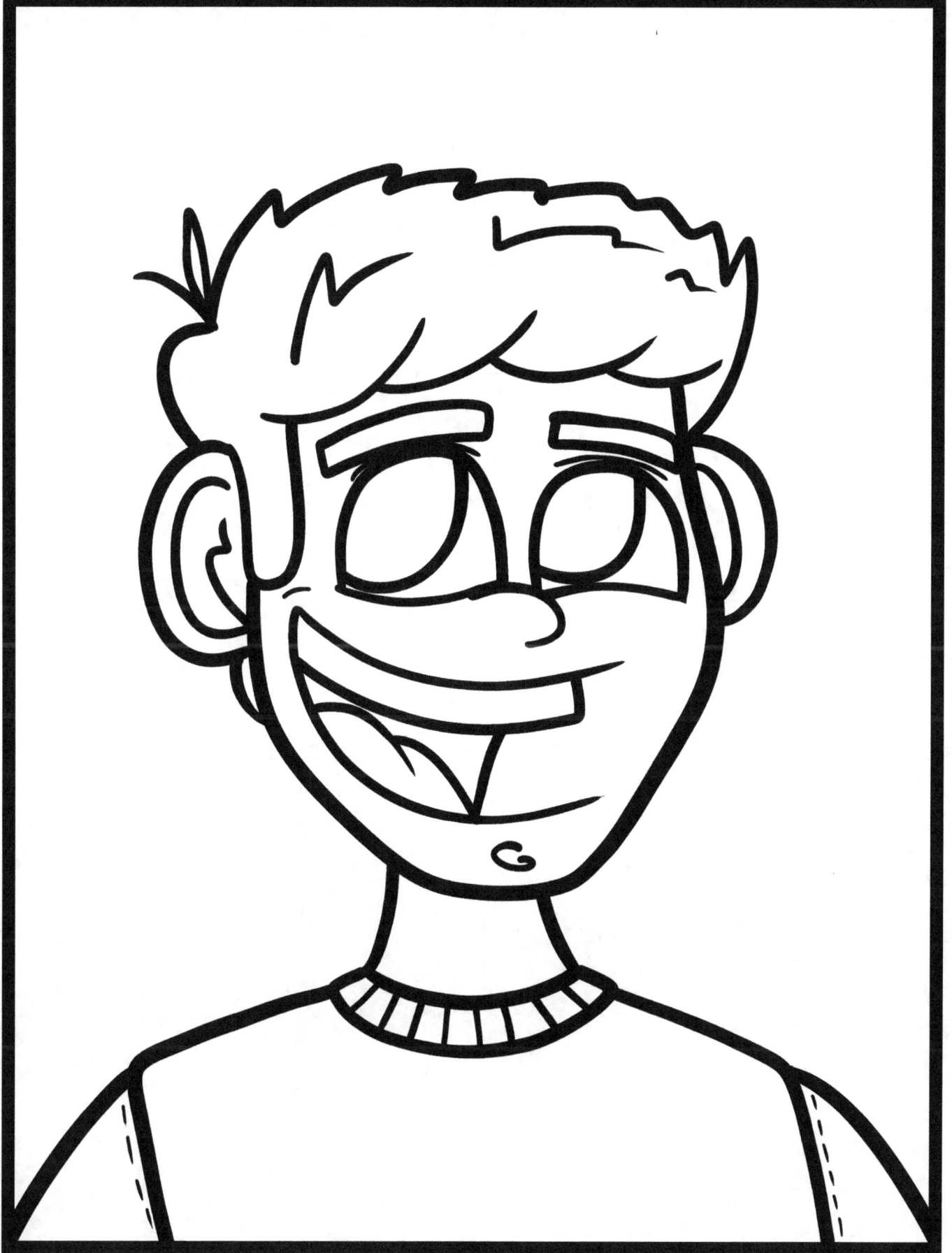

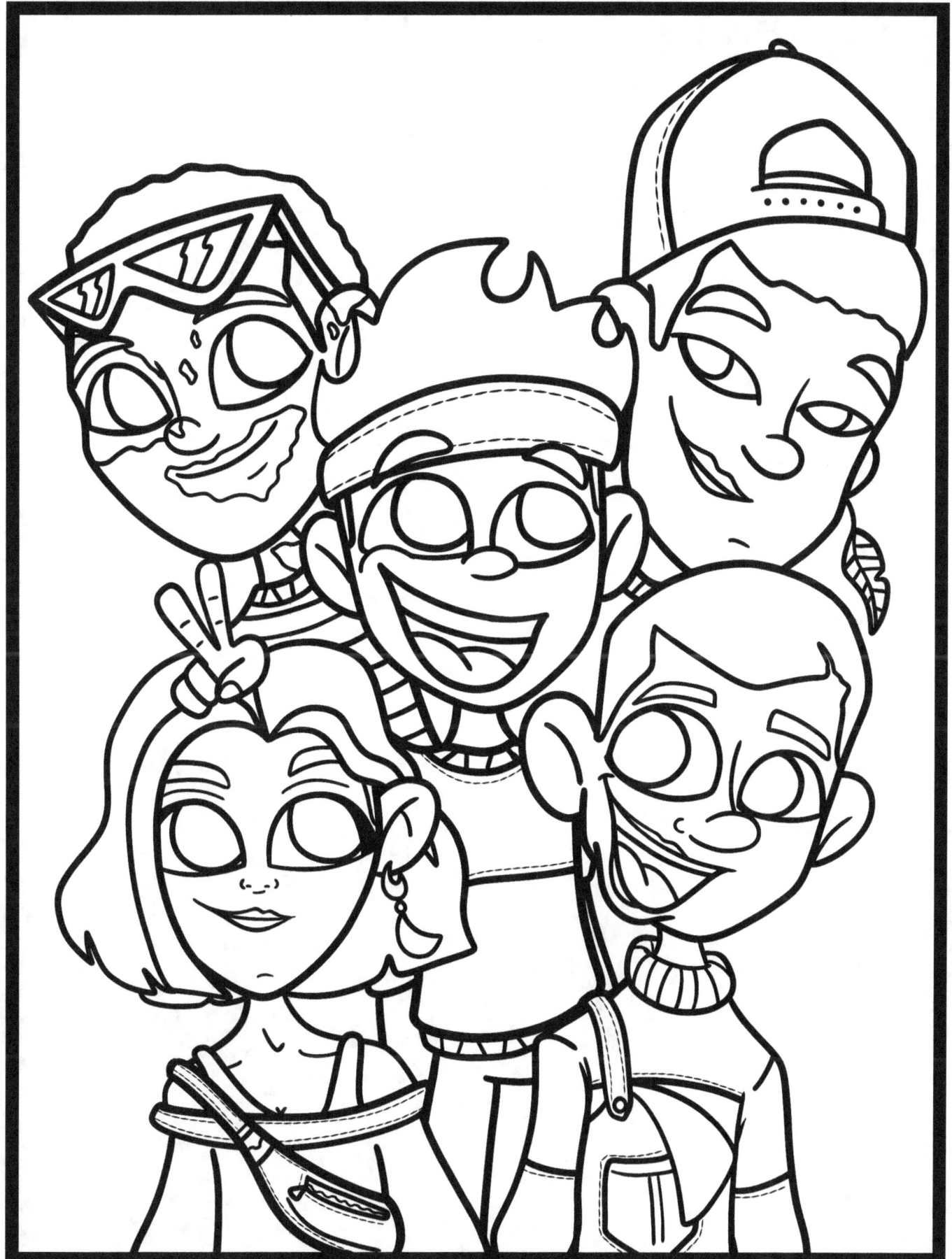

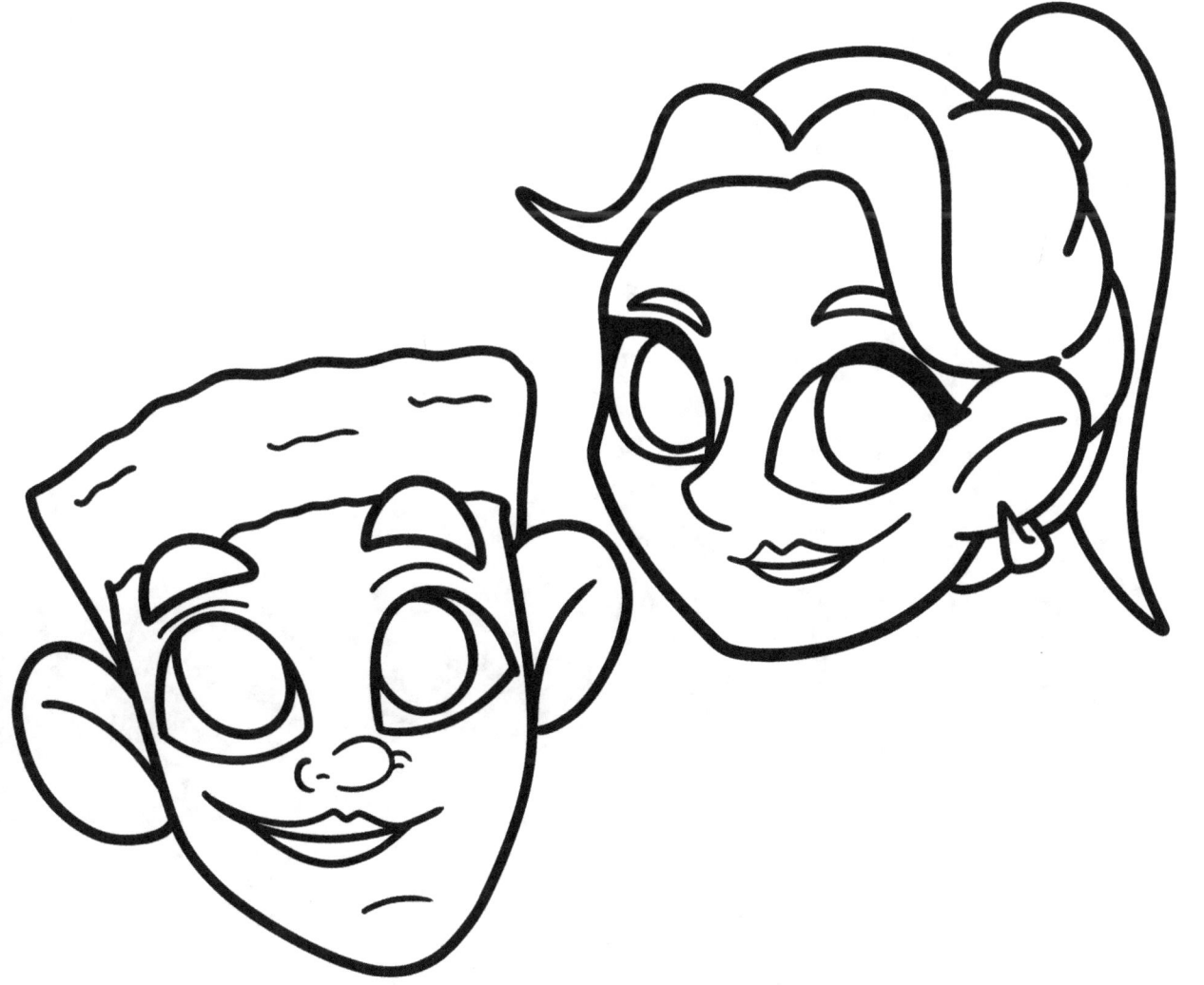

Share your colored pages to the
world by tagging me on them and
using the hashtags #FACESColors,
#alexcarrilloart and #alexcarrillo

I will share them on my social media
platforms.

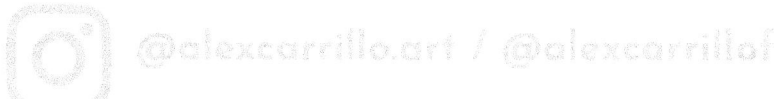 @alexcarrillo.art / @alexcarrillof

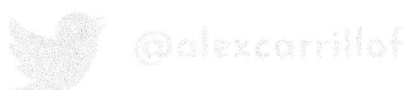 @alexcarrillof

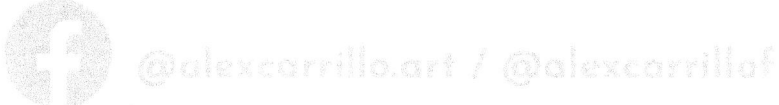 @alexcarrillo.art / @alexcarrillof

I hope you enjoyed FACES.

See you soon...

- Alex Carrillo

www.ingramcontent.com/pod-product-compliance
Lightning Source LLC
Chambersburg PA
CBHW081516220526
45467CB00010B/2944